THE LIFE IN RESEARCH

Some recollections of those who have known it,
and some insights for those who may
like to know more

Collected and Edited by
Peter Bartram

Grosvenor House
Publishing Limited

This book is published by
Grosvenor House Publishing Ltd
Link House
140 The Broadway, Tolworth, Surrey, KT6 7HT.
www.grosvenorhousepublishing.co.uk

A CIP record for this book
is available from the British Library

ISBN 978-1-83975-454-8

All proceeds from sales of this volume will be donated to the Archive of Market and Social Research which is the guardian and principal source of the whole history of the research industry. To know more about this Registered Charity, and support it whether by helping as a volunteer, contributing material, or making a financial donation, see www.amsr.org.uk

This book is inspired in part by Dame Judi Dench who, in conversation with one of the authors in a local pub, asked what he did for a living. When he replied "mostly market research" she immediately retorted: "what's that?"

This book aims to provide an answer for her and for anyone else unfamiliar with a profession which plays such a significant role in the life of the nation.

Note 1: It is fully recognised that some of the stories and anecdotes contained in this book may offend 21st Century sensibilities, but they are included in order to provide a true reflection of the mischievous, unthinking and privileged ways some people acted and expressed themselves in earlier unenlightened times.

Note 2: We have tried to secure permission from the cartoonists and/or publications shown in this book, and in most cases this has been freely granted, recognising this is a charity project. But since nearly all of the cartoons were originally published 30+ years ago, it has not been achievable in every case.

Contents

Acknowledgements

The impetus for creating all that follows was originally the inspiration of Paul Walton, while its content was assembled (despite the restrictions of Covid-19) by Peter Bartram from contributions generously provided by many others with relevant UK experience stretching back over the last 50 years. In the 125 personal stories and anecdotes included here, we have endeavoured always to ensure that everything written is true, but if any are misconstrued, the fault is ours and apologies are due.

Special thanks should be expressed towards:

- Doreen Blythe, for permission to use excerpts from her late husband Ian's book 'The Making of an Industry', and Colin Mc Donald for permission to use information contained in his book entitled 'Sampling the Universe'. These books are the most authoritative accounts of the history of the Market Research Society and its industry, at least until 1985.
- The Research Network, chaired by Adam Phillips, whose Newsletters from 2002 onwards contain stories from the past, many of which are taken from the MRS Newsletter and Research Magazine over the years.
- Sue Robson and her round-table discussion group which included Roula Bardawil, Anne Brister, Fiona Davies-Baker, Rebecca Harrison, Clare Mansfield, Kevin McLean, Catherine Millican, John Rose, Sarah Taylor, Judith Wardle, and Frances Yelland.
- Marie-Lise Audley, for permission to use her late father's cartoons.
- Others sharing their stories, including Tess Alps, Michael Ashfield, Jane Bain, Ken Baker, Phil Barnard, John Barter, Simon Chadwick, Louise Cretton, Jackie Dickens, Stephen Ellis, Mervyn Flack, Roger Gane, John Kearon, John Kelly, Derek Simonds, Nigel Spackman, Humphrey Taylor, Graham Woodham and, not least, the late Mary Reilly Bartram.
- Those who have also provided advice on the content, including Jane Frost, Danny Russell, Rossanne Lee-Bertram, Shirley Brent, Jacob Bartram, John Kearon, Sue Robson and Bill Blyth.

Foreword: The Past was a Foreign Country

Take yourself back to 1961: you are sitting in a country pub where the slow-moving barman will serve you drinks but, since it is not in his job description, not food. He tells you the food waiter might serve you when he gets back from his lunch "if you are lucky".

At the other end of the bar sits a journalist down from London aiming to report authoritatively on local opinion in the light of an upcoming by-election.

Across town, the shops close on Sundays, there's early closing on Wednesday afternoons, and the banks close on every weekday at 3.00pm.

Now step forward to 2020 (at least, before Covid-19): in the pub, you will get what you want from any of the bar staff, and quickly; the journalist's claim to know local opinion is challenged by a representative opinion survey; most service organisations are open at the weekend and your encounter with any one of them may conclude with a request that you complete a customer satisfaction questionnaire.

In short, across our national life, a production-oriented approach has given way to market-driven thinking in which the expectations and needs of customers determine the ways in which products and services are delivered to them.

And what has prompted this revolution in national life? The answer is that, more than almost anything else, the imperatives of representative survey research have driven the process. No longer will the barman serve you with surly reluctance; the lone journalist can no longer claim to measure opinion reliably, and the shops, banks and other high street outlets will stay open at more times when their customers may need them.

1. THE RESEARCH INDUSTRY AND ITS PEOPLE

The Birth of the Research Industry.

The technical origins of market research may be said to have been derived from the sampling procedures utilised in the 19th century and even earlier by the agricultural and medical professions, and also in pioneer advertising agencies in the USA, testing new developments and identifying what works best. Then at the beginning of the 20th century this began to be adapted in the UK to population studies, to advertising and packaged consumer goods, and to social issues such as those explored by Tom Harrisson and Charles Madge when they founded Mass Observation and surveyed public morale during the second world war.

Henry Durant, (founder of the UK Gallup company) later reported that "The second world war was an exciting time to be doing market research. The Gallup Poll, published in the New Chronicle, never missed a week, and it found that Lord Haw-Haw was most effective when he told truths not released by the government. Meanwhile Mark Abrams was busy doing content analysis on Goebbels' propaganda, and measuring the effect of German heavy bombing on civilian behaviour." Desk research is not like that any more.

Thereafter, acceptance of the validity of the sampling, questioning and reporting techniques was recognised across a widening range of industries. In the years after the second world war, manufacturers wanted to test reactions to their products, media owners wanted to prove to advertisers how many readers, viewers or listeners they could attract. And politicians, governments, and social services both locally and nationally, needed to measure public perceptions, needs and moods. The travel industry probably came next, wanting to test new service ideas and reactions to their holiday or journey experiences. They were followed in the 1970s by the banks and other financial services.

Finally in the 1980s professional services such as accountancy and law broke with their cultural assumption that they knew their clients' needs better than the clients themselves, and began to take a greater interest in their expectations.

"I think we should have done more market research."
PUNCH *JUNE 2 1989*

For those who have participated in this revolution by providing the research which underpinned it, it has been an exciting voyage of discovery. But from the outside, it may have been seen as a nerdy, desk-bound, numbers-oriented career, and this perception has perhaps been reinforced by the most recent growth of electronic data collection and massive data banks endlessly massaged for market insights.

But we hope to show that this has not been the case: the world of research is full of human-interest stories and motivational insights of interest to anyone, no matter how unfamiliar they may be with it. For those who may be considering a career path in research, it shows that this is a working life which is varied, challenging, enjoyable, ethically beneficial, and worthwhile. And for those aiming to move on eventually to a career in marketing, advertising, social services or general management, the skills learned in research also make it a relevant and worthwhile starting point.

This account will not cover the dry technical developments which have been described by many others, but rather the people, places and situations which such a life can provide.

From the anecdotes included in this volume it might be supposed that researchers over the last 50 years cared little for the accuracy and validity of their work. But that has not been the case. They enjoyed the life in research, but their technical standards were rigorous.

The Market Research Society

The MRS has always been the main professional body to which all proper researchers will wish to belong. According to one of its early founders, Mark Abrams, "it was born in 1946 out of a lunch I had with Robert Silvey who was then at the BBC, and Jack Haydock, head of the advertising agency Masius Ferguson. One of us said "Now there are three of us why don't we have a Society?" and we said 'Yes, fine, but who else is there?" Well, we found Olaf Ellefsen, Bernard Attwood and Henry Durant and we ended up with seven. We drew lots for who should be Chairman, and Henry won."

The Society was then set up more formally by a meeting of 23 founder Members on 5th September 1946. Of these, only 4 were women – though by 1986, among MRS Members generally (of which there then were 5,500) this proportion had risen to 48%, and by 2019 as many as 52% were women.

The authority of the MRS has always been sustained by its Code of Conduct, its educational programmes, and by its publications and promotional events, including its Annual Conference held every year in March. For anyone with a career in market research, which usually entails several changes of employer and role, it remains the reassuring and constant source of guidance and support on how to conduct one's research activities.

Lord Kearton, President of the MRS, speaking at the Annual Conference in 1984, gave confidence and encouragement to all researchers by asserting "market research has moved rightly to professional status: it has an admissions system, an educational system, and qualification procedures. It is an indispensible link in the chain of wealth-creating activities in our society."

From its beginnings in 1946 membership of the MRS grew fast: it had reached 2,500 by 1976, and 5,500 by 1986; and then it peaked at more than 8,000 around the turn of the century, after which there has been a decline to the current level of around 5,000. In 1946 34% of the members were from advertising agencies, but by 1985 this proportion declined to 7% as more and more research suppliers and buyers wished to take up membership.

The decline in membership since the start of the 21st century has occurred despite the robust growth of the industry as a whole, and may in part be due to the establishment of the MRS Company Partner scheme in 2005. 500+ companies now participate, and this may have led many researchers to feel more protected by their employer's participation and absolved of their individual professional responsibilities.

The Market Research Industry

Before being afflicted by the onset of coronavirus, the turnover of the UK research industry in 2019 stood at well over £4 billion and it employed 73,000 people, many of whom worked for the 300+ research suppliers large and small. At £77 per head of population per annum, no country on earth spent more on market and social research activities.

> *Nevertheless, your chances of being interviewed in any UK nationwide survey of, say, 1,000 adults are less than one in 50,000. And even if 1,000 such surveys are conducted in any year, there's only a chance of one in fifty that you will be interviewed.*

Globally, the research industry was valued in 2017 at $76 billion, of which the USA accounted for 44% and the UK came second at 14%. Of this global total, 81% was spent on larger-sample quantitative studies and only 14% on in-depth qualitative interviews and focus groups which, being based on smaller numbers of participants, cost relatively less but are widely undertaken. The big trend in recent years has been towards automation and big data: in the UK 88% of research agencies had used on-line surveys in the last 12 months, while 60% had undertaken or commissioned focus groups; and one of their main preoccupations has been the need to conform with government GDPR regulations.

A survey conducted by one leading research company among the general public in 1979 found 59% saying market research is 'a good thing' with only 3% actively disagreeing. 79% said they had not been contacted by market researchers before, but 20% had been subjected to 'Sugging' (Selling Under the Guise of Market Research). After considerable argument, in 1977 an Interviewer Card Scheme had been launched, in order to reinforce the bona fide credentials of interviewers. When contacting possible respondents, each interviewer could show a card with her (or his) name, photo and signature on it.

Then in 2019, the GRBN Global Trust Survey of 10 countries included the UK, where it was found there was a widespread lack of trust in various information sources: 53% of UK adults did not trust social media companies, 44% said the same of media companies, and 33% of data analysis companies. In such an environment, it is more encouraging that only 21% said they did not trust market research companies, and 63% could see the benefits of MR to businesses.

> • *Such has been the growth of this industry, that it has penetrated all aspects of national life: as early as December 1979 the Financial Times received a letter from a reader who wrote: "Answering my front door last night, I was confronted by two small boys asking me to name two favourite carols. "A bit early for carols isn't it?" I asked. "We're not going to sing now lady" they replied. "We're doing market research."*

As the MRS grew, more Members felt the need for their own type of activity to be catered for, and this led to the creation of specialised interest groups such as IMRA (the Industrial Market Research Association, in 1963), AURA (the Association of Users of Research Agencies, in 1965), and AQRP (the Association of Qualitative Research Practitioners, in 1982).In 1976 the Market Research Benevolent Association (MRBA) was founded, to provide financial help to researchers (mostly interviewers) who fell on hard times.

The Purposes of Research

Many of those unfamiliar with the research industry, or new to it, do not realise how varied are the purposes for which research can be undertaken. They may have encountered customer satisfaction surveys (or at least customer cards inflicted on every restaurant customer and pop-up questionnaires after every on-line purchase); and they may have been involved in focus groups or new product tests or research on new advertising ideas (usually conducted by gathering in a central location such as a village hall), or omnibus surveys which may cover about ten different subjects in the one interview. Some of these projects are completed without the interaction of an interviewer, using a self-completion questionnaire administered by each participant either on paper or on-line, as is the case with many of these:

- The whole field of media audience measurement surveys,
- Basic market surveys which often incorporate a segmentation of people according to their characteristics or preferences, or identify the channels by which products or services should be delivered.
- Especially in mature markets, very large tracking surveys or panels in which changes over time can be measured accurately.
- Large-scale audits undertaken in order to measure the through-put of goods in retail stores, and
- Mystery shopping, using an interviewer to simulate the experiences of customers.

The exception is qualitative research which, with some exceptions, still relies largely on in-person contact.

These activities are not only generated by the needs of commercial organisations, but also entail social research answering the needs of national government departments, local governments, charities and other foundations, such as those connected to the medical profession. Among many examples of such surveys have been those needed to test and keep abreast of developments related to Covid-19, and those covering specific catchment areas of individual Hospital Trusts. Past examples have included surveys for The London Hospital in the East End, for the King Edward VII Hospital near Midhurst in West Sussex; and one nationwide survey was undertaken to measure the incidence and causes of hypothermia among the elderly: this required interviewers not only to administer a structured questionnaire, but also to take the core body temperatures of the elderly participants.

Characteristics of Researchers

In the past, it has seemed that many of the people attracted to a career in market research tended to be reserved rather than extrovert, and book-smart rather than street-smart in the manner associated more with those in advertising or marketing. This led one observer to describe researchers in 1982 as "honest but cautious, introverted and lacking flair" and another to write in 1985 that they were "given to introspection ... as much fascinated by their discipline and methodologies as in giving clients an answer". All the signs are that that has now changed.

Certainly they tended to be brainy: a survey of Market Research Society Members in 1972 found that 72% had some kind of degree, their leading subjects being economics (48%), statistics (20%) and psychology (17%). Increasingly there has been more gender equality among them than in most other professions: at the start, in 1953, only 8% of them were women, but this increased to 22% in 1971, to 48% in 1986, and to 52% in 2019, with many companies run by women. The first woman to be voted Chairman of the MRS was Eileen Cole in 1972; she has been followed in later years by several others, and the current CEO of the MRS is Jane Frost CBE.

The notion that researchers were, or are, desk-bound nerds is refuted by a 'Who's Who in Research' volume compiled in 1985. Participants were asked to describe their interests and one random practitioner listed 'Motoring, opera, wine, food, travel, English 19th Century watercolours, and beautiful women'. Others offered 'jazz music, real ale', 'retired footballer', 'voluntary service as a Gentleman of the Chapel Royal, Hampton Court Palace', and 'Commissioned Officer in the Seaforth Highlanders and Assistant Keeper of Printed Books at the British Museum'. And one director of a leading research company has also been the musical director for several pop stars.

"Market research is merely what I do. It's not where I am."

> • As an example of this infinite variety, in 1978 the head of one leading research company was described as *"extremely ambitious, exceptionally clever, desperately ill-organised, ...only marginally devious, can walk down a flight of stairs on his hands, is an unfailingly interesting conversationalist, and altogether a bit of a sweetie."*

Anyone aiming to start a career in this industry can be assured that the various routes into it have always been, and remain (once we have recovered from the virus-induced recession), relatively accessible. There are 300+ research companies to choose from, all listed in the annual Research Buyers' Guide, and otherwise there are plenty of research-buying organisations with specialist research departments. Although the recruitment processes of the largest companies tend to be very formal, for many others they may not be.

- *One senior researcher, looking back on his working life has said: "Only once in my career did a job result from any formal interview and selection process. As the industry is mostly made up of many small companies, their recruitment processes are often informal, and it is mainly a question of timing, and seizing opportunities as soon as they arise. It is worth calling any company to ask if they have any current vacancies – at any level, whether interviewing, coding or other administration. Once inside, you can learn quickly, roles are changeable and progress can be fast."*

"Well, Mr Cody, according to our questionnaire, you would probably excel in sales, advertising, slaughtering a few thousand buffalo, or market research"

- In 1985 one leading qualitative researcher said that colleagues and clients could be categorised as either 'radiators' or 'drains', to distinguish those she wanted to work with from those she did not.

Executive Life

While those who join a small or qualitative-orientated business are quickly pitched into interviewing and other responsibilities, in larger companies those who do not join via interviewing usually begin their careers in research as an office-bound trainee executive, learning the methods used in the various departments contributing to the whole research process. Maybe not immediately but soon after, one may be trusted to perform in a presentation of the results to a client.

As recalled by one of the industry's elder statesmen, this pattern was established right from the beginning of the industry. In 1948 he joined a leading research company, and on his first morning was asked to help in analysing a survey for the Boy Scouts Association. These kinds of department may no longer exist, but, the next day he worked in the Charting Department and this was quickly followed by short periods in the Computer Section, the Retail Audit Tabulation Section and the Field Department (where the manager liked to hire Scots or Australians with their class-neutral accents). Finally, after this complete round of training sessions, his first job as an executive was on a survey of boot polishes for the Cherry Blossom Company.

Internal Politics: While new recruits can expect support and guidance from experienced colleagues, in the early days when the unions were all-powerful and managements correspondingly weak, securing cooperation from the various production departments necessitated strong negotiating skills and inducements:

> • *In one leading company, junior executives found that dating a girl in the charting department much improved their chances of jumping the queue of work in their in-tray. In the fieldwork department, booking work necessitated perilous negotiation with the all-powerful director, a fearsome lady*

> *who was also a retired senior police officer. And in the data analysis department it was found that the Irish computer manager could become much more compliant after being treated to two pints of Guinness.*

In the sixties when our military institutions were once again being reduced in size, their personnel were being retired and were forced to find employment in 'civvy street'. Several research companies saw them as good disciplined managers and provided them with jobs in their production departments, though this did not always work successfully:

> • *One leading research company recruited a recently retired senior RAF officer who began work with the expectation, drawn from his service life, that when he asked one of their young Cockney printers to do something, he would be obeyed instantly. He was shocked to receive the immediate response "Get stuffed and f**k off" and, realising that there was going to be an unbridgeable culture clash, left the company soon after.*

While most worked hard and with professional precision, the life in research could include some riotous behaviour of a kind rarely to be seen nowadays.

For instance, several research companies always held lively Christmas parties for their employees:

> • *The party at one leading company was described as "fuelled by booze and sex" and in one year the head of the company arrived at his office on the Monday morning following the party held on the previous Friday, only to find that his large and elegant glass desk had split in two and fallen to the floor. Further inspection revealed that the culprit had left visible evidence behind: on the glass was the perfect print of a pair of buttocks.*

It seems clear that 90% of all that one needs to know for a career in market research is learned in the first two years, especially if one is guided by a senior colleague able to show how the best design intentions can fall apart when tested against survey respondents or statistical theory. And it is remarkable how durable the attachments in one's first research job can be: you can remain friendly 50 years later with those you worked with at that time.

> • *Another minor escapade occurred when a junior research executive working in a small office shared with his young secretary at a leading newspaper group sat on the corner of a metal desk and inadvertently tore a large hole in the seat of his trousers. The secretary immediately said "Quick, there's no-one around. Give them to me and I will stitch them together for you." So he took off his trousers and calmly carried on writing a report at his desk. At which point there was a surprise visitation by the young son and heir of the great proprietor, Lord X, keen to know more about "what you research chaps are getting up to." For fear of revealing his trouserless state, the young executive failed to get up to greet his visitor, but conducted a ten-minute conversation on technical methods while the secretary sat across the room, suppressing her giggles. Thankfully the visitor soon left, never knowing that he had conversed with the young executive in his underpants.*

Sound advice and reassurance for any young person starting out on the supplier side of this profession, if not elsewhere, is offered by one experienced researcher:

- Be prepared to take responsibility and be ready to step in
- Know that most directors will support you no matter what
- Listen, listen, listen – the senior researchers are worth listening to

- Methodology – don't just take the client's word for it, make sure it's the right one for the project and takes in to account all its idiosyncrasies
- Fieldwork is where anything can happen, so be prepared
- The client is not always right, but may need convincing of that sometimes, especially regarding their target market
- Clients are not all bad.
- Culture is key – make sure you understand what goes on in a different culture, it could impact your project and even your liberty - and brush up on the local lingo!
- The respondent is always right, even when they are clearly wrong – perception is reality.
- Ethnography has its boundaries…you can end up being just TOO close.
- Alcohol is our enemy – even when we're researching alcohol.
- Stimulus material must be carefully supervised & managed at all times.
- Etiquette – know your boundaries but don't be afraid to push them on occasion.

Social Activities

In the 1980s and 1990s, the most robust period of the Market Research Society's growth, all sorts of social groups were formed under its banner. In 1985 these covered sports such as:

- Cricket, with a match against the Government Statistical Service,
- A Squash competition and a Badminton tournament,
- A Bridge competition (held at the Charing Cross Hotel),
- A Snooker competition (at the King's Cross Snooker and Social Club),
- An MRS Golf Day held at the RAC Country Club, Epsom,
- And later, Darts and a Sports Quiz.

In 1984 as many as 1,000 Members and their guests attended the Society's Christmas Lunch at the Royal Lancaster Hotel, attracted by the guest speakers Mel Smith and Griff Rhys-Jones. In previous years such guest speakers included Bob Monkhouse (1965), Clement Freud (1967), Dick Emery (1968), and Michael Bentine (1976). And the Society's Annual Luncheons were addressed by political luminaries including Harold Wilson, Michael Heseltine, Shirley Williams and Tim Bell.

In 1981, an inaugural riverboat trip was organised, for which 170 revellers boarded the 'Nautica' at Lambeth Pier and sailed downstream to the Thames Barrier and back. It was an atmosphere described as 'non-pushy' where "friends were able to talk with no hint of the nasty commercialism one sometimes sees. At £6 a head, it was a bargain .... nicely timed to fill that tiresome gap between the Derby and Wimbledon."

Since then, as in many other professions, the life in research seems to have become more serious, and apart from the Annual Awards Dinner held in November each year, few of these social activities are offered today.

In that period of robust growth, it appears that Members' wish to be involved in the Society was also at its greatest: for instance, in 1979 as many as 134 were concerned to attend the Society's Annual General Meeting. Maybe the contentious issues no longer need to be discussed and there is greater confidence in the Society's Secretariat and Board, but nowadays the MRS AGM is more likely to be attended by 30 Members or fewer.

But the ability of the Society, and the industry as a whole, to promote and demonstrate the value of its work to the outside world has always been questioned. In 1973, the then Chairman of the MRS wrote "What market research is largely about is information and communication. So it is perhaps not surprising that, in the tradition of the shoemaker's barefoot children, this is an area where we have not particularly excelled." *No longer true?*

2. THE RESEARCH PROCESS

The Typical Project Sequence

Though many young researchers are nowadays involved solely in big data massaging operations at one extreme, and smaller qualitative research projects at the other, most exploratory full-service projects are based on contacting respondents and involve a similar sequence of activities:

- First there must be a client organisation wanting answers to questions about its target market, and willing to pay for them.
- They should prepare a brief describing their needs, perhaps suggesting methods thought most appropriate. Unless a positive and continuing relationship has been established with a preferred supplier, the brief may be sent out to 2-4 research companies, asking for proposals and costings. The choice of these would often be restricted to those approved in advance by the Procurement or Purchasing Department.
- The chosen company will then need to know where and how to select participants without bias, perhaps using a list or other source (such as of its customers, or the electoral register)
- They will devise a questionnaire or topic guide for small scale qualitative research; or for a larger project, a draft which should be tested in a short pilot study in preparation for a main quantitative stage which follows.
- Interviewers will be briefed on the fieldwork requirements, and set individual targets for the number and types of respondent to be contacted.
- When all interviewing is done, whether in person, by phone, via I-Pads or on the internet, supervisors should do some back-checking to ensure good quality, and the results

delivered incorporating cross-analyses devised by the research executive in consultation with the client.

- Finally an in-person presentation of the results will be delivered together with insights and recommendations as to the actions which should follow. In earlier days this would be preceded or followed by a detailed report, but nowadays this is often omitted, as a set of Powerpoint presentation slides is thought sufficient.

There are many variations on this process and, not least, as we shall see, much can go wrong and much amusement derived from the mishaps which can occur.

In the MRS Newsletter in 1992, a lighthearted competition to devise definitions which might be included in a new edition of the Dictionary of Market Research was won by a reader who offered the following terminological (in)exactitudes:

Focus Group Discussion: Trying to get the answer the ad agency wants.

Snowballing: Looking for a respondent you haven't got a snowball's chance in hell of finding.

Social research: 'What are you doing after work?'

Image battery: Opinion polls' effect on politicians.

Adding Value (as in a research proposal): "We're competing against a bloody management consultancy again."

Harmonisation: The art of persuading people who speak foreign languages that our way is right.

Interviewing Experiences

It is anyway very worthwhile to begin a career in research as an interviewer (of which there are 20,000 nationally nowadays), mainly because it helps to ensure later on as an executive that one is less likely to inflict on interviewers (and the public) questionnaires and project tasks unrelated to practical realities.

The work of an interviewer, braving all weathers, not very well paid, and dealing with difficult quota categories and over-long questionnaires, can seem tedious, whether face to-face with the public or in a telephone call centre.

But encounters with the public can be stimulating and at times very amusing, especially in the many situations in which research executives inflict impossible tasks on fieldworkers:

- *In a questionnaire dreamed up by some office-bound executive, one little old lady was asked "Do you think Britain should have her own independent nuclear deterrent, or shelter under the American nuclear umbrella?" She replied: "No, I've got an umbrella, don't need another one."*

- *And conducting a by-election survey in remote west Perthshire, similar questions about political issues were often rebutted with "Aye, well, we've got a good Laird, he'll be knowing about that"*

- *The unexpected can sometimes occur, as when an interviewer asked to speak with a Mr Jones, and received the reply "Certainly dear, come on in." When she was shown in to the front room, she was greeted the sight of a large coffin containing the deceased Mr Jones.*

- *On another occasion, the interviewer was told by a family member concerning the lady she was seeking that "she's queer in bed under the doctor."*

"Fancy a bit of research, luv?"

- *The requirement to seek out people of a particular type can in some cases present unusual difficulty. When a leading brand of men's jeans was launching a new product, they needed to check the fit and style in the zip area. Both male and female interviewers were required to accost men in the street and ask them to come in and be measured in their underwear.*

- *On another occasion, a nervous young male research executive had to ask interviewers to recruit three categories of respondent for a study of San Pro tampons. His field manager had to educate him by explaining how women could experience heavy, medium or light flow during the menstrual cycle. He was very embarrassed, but later surprised to find that participants in each category had been recruited very easily.*

- *Research among the most affluent respondents is often required, particularly by financial institutions and among leaders of businesses both large and small. One such study was undertaken among its owners for a luxury car manufacturer, and this included an in-home depth interview with an owner in Mayfair who started by saying how useful his Bentley was, adding "and by the way I also have 35 Land Rovers at my rural home. They are useful too." And a senior banker similarly interviewed volunteered "I like to drive my Rolls Royce to my local fish and chip shop as it enables me to present a virtual two fingers to any other customer who gives me a funny look." Another world exposed.*

There is also a darker side to life which many researchers encounter:

- *A fresh young 22-year-old researcher conducting interviews on long-term unemployment was sent to a rough estate in the north-east of England. Towards the end of her day, she knocked at the door of a tower block flat and on entering found the whole family sitting there in candlelight – there was no money for 'the electric'. A deeply sad interview followed – they had run out of everything, including hope.*

- *In the 1970s a graduate trainee was sent to a run-down council estate with feral dogs, and rubbish everywhere ... She managed to get 20 interviews in the area, but at one house she was invited into the kitchen, where sat a large man in a vest and trousers who had clearly had too much to drink. Fortunately his wife was also there, but it soon became evident that neither of them could read, so it was no use trying to get their reactions to show-cards.*

- *On another occasion, a project involved interviewing people who were incapacitated in some way – by old age, disability or injury – and the interviewer had to go to a similarly run-down part of southwest London. With her supervisor saying "Call me if you encounter the slightest hint of trouble" she entered a high rise building which reeked of urine and had no lift. She interviewed a young man in his 20s in his very untidy living room, and left immediately.*

- *A research agency was conducting social research and needed to seek out unemployed people with no bank account. Knocking on one door in Leeds, the homeowner thought the interviewer was 'from the social', pulled a knife on her and chased her down the front path.*

Even within the UK, translation and dialect problems can occur. The head of one leading research company recalls that in in the area around King's Lynn where there are many agricultural workers from eastern Europe, it is useful to have a Polish language version of your questionnaire; and in the more distant parts of Wales a Welsh language version will also be needed.

Even in parts of Scotland the English language itself can be a mystery to interviewers and focus group convenors from Down South:

- *In Aberdeen a local researcher offered this message to a colleague: "Am goin doon the pea dower the cundie to the store ta get ma messages." Not understood.*

- *And during a group session in Glasgow participants were shown an advertisement for a brand of whisky which included some quotes from Shakespeare in order to try to reinforce the brand image. There followed a long silence, until one man spoke up: "Jimmy willne ken that". Another participant, an Englishman living in Glasgow, then said to the convenor "You didn't understand that did you?" and explained that it meant the average Scotsman (ie Jimmy) would not understand what the ad was trying to say. Needless to say, the ad was withdrawn by the client.*

- *Back in 1967, it was already known that sherry was more popular in Scotland than elsewhere in the UK, and particularly sweet sherry among C2DE women. A sherry taste test was set up in a centrally located hall in Edinburgh, the participants seemingly including a preponderance of cleaning ladies. One of them became so exasperated with the questions asked of her that she finally snapped: "Och, shut up laddie and give me another sherry!" She was not to be denied.*

"Would you say Attila is doing an excellent job, a good job, a fair job or a poor job?"

Drawing by Charles Adams: © 1982. The New Yorker Magazine. Inc.

Reprinted from Public Opinion October/November 1983.

Nevertheless it is surprising what people will and won't agree to in the interview situation. One of the earliest pioneers in financial market research recalls that 30% or more would refuse to answer questions about their income, while in a survey of national sexual habits undertaken for the Sunday Times by one of his colleagues, people were happy, indeed keen, to describe what they got up to and refusals were less than 5%.

"Jean... if you could fill in this questionnaire on how you've enjoyed the evening."

Lest it be thought that interviewing is all a hard grind searching for respondents and taking abuse from interviewees, we should add that in most cases it is enjoyable.

> • *One experienced Field Director, asking several interviewers why they had chosen this kind of work, received the reply "So why, oh why, do we go on? Well, my husband's theory is that we are all curtain peepers. We just love to ask questions of perfect strangers that we would never dare to ask of even our nearest and dearest."*

Telephone and On-line Interviewing:

By the beginning of the 1980s, telephone research was becoming a significant activity, and by the end of the 1980s it was the leading data collection method in terms of number of interviews.

But in its early days the MRS rejected it as a proper data collection method, because it did not conform with its Code of Conduct which, until it was changed, was designed solely for in-person interviewing.

> • *A difficulty also arose in the early days from the fact that telephone interviewers could not be seen by the interviewees. In one of the early call centres there was a 6ft tall cross-dressing man, happily accepted by the team as 'Gloria'. On a project for a cosmetics company, the client insisted that all the interviewers must be female which as far as the team were concerned included 'Gloria'. Listening in to some of the telephone interviews, the client took exception to Gloria's definite masculine tones. This was in the days before wide acceptance of gender fluidity, and some rather difficult explanations were required.*

In 1983 it was reported that, as a method of interviewing the public, telephone interviewing had grown in terms of amount spent on it, from 2% to 23% of all forms of fieldwork, mostly by using Computer Assisted Telephone Interviewing systems (CATI). It then grew substantially, peaking in the first decade of the 21st century.

Thus by 1999 face-to-face interviewing still accounted for over 50% of expenditure on ad hoc market research but telephone was by far the most common form of interviewing (the cost per interview being much higher for face-to-face than telephone). The 21st century also saw the introduction of online interviewing in the USA and then elsewhere in the world and both face-to-face and telephone interviewing declined from around 2008 and online took over.

"I'm not trying to sell you anything, sir. I'm doing market research, and all I ask is two or three hours of your time to answer a few thousand questions."

THE NEW YORKER, MARCH 6, 2000

Questionnaire Design Issues

There can be no question that whatever changes are introduced by new technology, the art of good questionnaire design has always been and will remain a vital skill for every researcher.

For those entering the research industry early in its growth, the principal training bible was a book on questionnaire design, 'The Art of Asking Questions' by the American Stanley L Payne. Written in the 1950s and drawing on US experience it is still relevant for UK researchers today.

He reported that as far back as 1936, a group of experts surveying research in the USA called question-wording the number one problem in opinion research. The sample of researchers was asked what they saw as the primary defect of commercial research. Their most frequently mentioned criticisms were:

	%
Improperly worded questionnaires	74
Faulty interpretations	58
Inadequacy of sample	52
Improper statistical methods	52
Presentation of results without supporting data	41

Peter Chisnall in his book on 'Marketing Research' discussed the avoidance of bias: for example, rather than asking "Would you rather use Lux Toilet Soap than any other toilet soap?" a less inflated response would be obtained by asking "What is your favourite toilet soap?"

In another book by Paul E Green and Donald S Tull, three very similar questions were asked of three matched samples, with differing results:

1. Do you think anything should be done to make it easier for people to pay hospital or doctors' bills? — 82% Yes.
2. 'Should' replaced by 'Could' — 77% Yes
3. 'Should' replaced by 'Might' — 63% Yes

Embarrassing questions often have to be negotiated carefully, and another American, Allen H Barton of the University of Chicago, illustrated ghoulishly some ways to get a better response. These are applicable to many other sensitive issues:

1. **The Casual Approach**: Do you happen to have murdered your wife?
2. **The Numbered Card:** Please could you read the number off this card which corresponds to what became of your wife?
   1. Natural Death
   2. I killed her
   3. Other (What?)
3. **The 'Everybody' Approach**: As you may know, many people are killing their wives these days. Do you happen to have killed yours?
4. **The 'Other People' Approach**: Do you know any people who have murdered their wives? How about you?

Above all, precision is required – these are words to be careful with:

"You"	Q: How many phone sets did you repair last week? (Me personally? Or our whole shop?)
"Daily"	(Which do you intend, five working days or all seven?)
"Now"	Q: "What kind of work are you doing now?" A: "I am answering your silly questions!"
"See"	Q: "When did you last see your dentist?" A: "Yesterday on the golf course".

"Where"	Q: Where did you read that?" A(i): "In this newspaper". A(ii): "At home in front of the fire". A(iii): "In an advertisement".
"More" and "Less":	Than what? Than a competing brand? Than previously? Than any of the other possible answers?
"A Majority"	This can only mean more than 50%. If less than 50% but more than any other answer, it can only be 'a plurality'.

Many more examples could be shown here, but hopefully these will be sufficient to show that questionnaire design requires great skill to avoid the many pitfalls which can arise.

From Technique to Application

In the early years, many leading researchers emerged from, and were heavily influenced by, the disciplines of academic life.

> • *In the seventies, one of the best research agencies, Research Services Ltd, moved from their previous location in central London to a characterless office block overlooking the dense traffic of northwest London. In response to a comment that this seemed to be at odds with their reputation for sophisticated academic quality, one of their most elegant ex-Oxbridge Directors replied "We like to think of ourselves as the Athens of the North Circular".*

One of the consequences of the meticulous nature of such researchers was that when the industry was closer to its infancy, there tended to be an understandable emphasis on developing and justifying the techniques on which its subsequent success came to be based.

So, in following the scientific method, there was a need to produce a treatise in which the reader must plough through the detailed evidence before the final conclusions could be reached. The processes of analysis were slow and laborious, and there was an emphasis on paper reporting rather than any in-person communication via a presentation of the results in a group meeting.

In the years since then, the emphasis has shifted from technique to application, from an academic to a journalistic style, and to the addition of oral and pictorial communication, and story-telling. In other words, as researchers so often recommend to their clients, there has been a move from a production-oriented to a market-oriented delivery. And no longer do clients judge the value of a project by the thickness of the report delivered.

Presenting the Results and Insights

So as the industry matured (and although there are many exceptions), aided by new technology in-person presentations usually come first nowadays and are the principal forum in which decisions are taken. Information is being communicated pictorially, usually by Powerpoint charts and diagrams, rather than solely by words and numbers – which often used to be crudely hand-written on acetates shown by an overhead projector. This change has all happened despite an assertion in 1980 by one of the leading gurus of the industry (to considerable dissent in a crowded meeting) that "Graphs, bar charts etc are for the ignorant."

It has to be said that most research presentations are completed successfully without mishaps, by researchers who have become more comfortable with the required skills than in the early days.

But it is the disasters which are the most memorable. Many researchers can recall occasions when the presenter turned up late, could not operate the slide projector, or talked for far too long, or the charts were illegible or too complicated; or when the senior client executive fell asleep, picked a fight, or walked out before the end.

> • *One mishap in which the researcher revealed insufficient knowledge and control over his equipment occurred during a presentation to the Co-op Management in Manchester. The projector had three lenses, and the first slide, showing demographics of the town of Basildon where their research had been conducted, showed itself to be burning like toast. Someone should have told the presenter to use slides made of heat-resistant glass.*

Often, the full report is relegated to the status of an afterthought, placed on file as a reference document for the future. The main summaries and recommendations are shown at the front where the most important and busiest readers want them, and the supporting details follow after, for study by those who wish to read further.

One leading researcher recalled in 2003 the advice on report writing that he had received from senior colleagues earlier in his career. They said:

o   Keep sentences short
o   Do not split infinitives
o   Write up boring market research findings like Earnest Hemingway, and
o   Use 'Fowler's Modern English Usage'.

He also recalled that when he wrote a learned 12-page article for the MRS Journal, it was professionally edited by a colleague/friend, who cut it down to three pages.

On reporting procedures, there has long been an argument among researchers as to whether one should merely report the findings as evidenced in the results, or add conclusions and insights based on the researcher's own experience.

Nowadays there is a keenness for researchers to abandon reticence by providing insights to top client managements. But as this shows, in the early days most researchers were reluctant to do that as it was assumed they would never know the client's business well enough to be credible:

> • *Early in 1974 at a joint meeting of MRS and Marketing Society members, called to discuss whether the market research reporting should include marketing and management advice. Both main speakers argued that the decision making process included other areas of management such as R&D, production, and sales, and since researchers rarely party to all of the client's problems, they are not in a first rate position to provide for realistic marketing decisions.*

Nevertheless, the impulse to provide advice as well as facts did sometimes come from the clients themselves:

> • *One early example of this arose when the results of research among financial institutions in the City of London were presented to a management team at IBM. They immediately asked the researcher to abandon diffidence and be bold, saying "If you can put together a dozen personal suggestions arising from this research, don't worry if most of them are naive or impractical – we will know what's realistic and if you, as an outsider, can offer only a couple of worthwhile ideas we have not considered, that would more than justify the amount we have spent in commissioning this project".*

However there does remain an obligation for the researcher to separate clearly what is derived from the research from what is based on personal experience:

> • *Sometimes the writer of a research report will inject into it his personal explanation of the findings, as happened in a report on as study of uses of bath additives such as Radox or Epsom salts. His report took as scientific fact that a large amount of Dettol would kill off unknown threats to your health and, seemingly influenced by Freud, he went on to suggest that women were using bath additives for psychological reasons rather than chemical protection. They felt naked and vulnerable in a bath, and a bath additive offered a safeguard against possible intrusion by a strange or unwelcome man.*

3. THE ACTORS AND ACTIVITIES

The Research Buyers

In the early days of the research industry, research activity was mostly dominated by the larger client organisations such as the General Foods, Gillette, Metal Box Company, Reckitt and Colman, Mars, Nestle, Thomas Lipton, Unilever, Procter and Gamble and the advertising agencies Garland Compton, Benton and Bowles, Foot, Cone and Belding, and Leo

"You say it's a market research problem, I say you're a lousy trumpet player ! "

Burnett. Their Research Managers were competent, knowledgeable and powerful. It was recognised that not all problems can be solved by market research, but their intellectual leadership was clear, and their choices were technically well-informed.

In those early days the research companies regularly entertained the buyers in what were described as *"lengthy liquid lunches in a haze of cigar smoke."*

> • *This was the era of taking clients to lunch, a long alcoholic affair, and work after lunch sometimes never happened. And one researcher recalled being taken by their clients to the park for a food and wine picnic (acquired by their secretaries). "Afterwards we took boats out on the Serpentine, where we finished the wine."*

> • *The lady owner of one of the largest research audit companies placed strong emphasis on stylish client entertainment, to the extent that employees were reprimanded if their entertainment expenses were not high enough. But her slightly lacklustre appearance apparently did not match with her regal aspirations, and when greeting clients arriving at a reception for clients which she was hosting at The Savoy, a lot of coats were dumped on her as she was taken to be the hat-check lady.*

> • *And one research company recalls that their accountant looked at their Petty Cash Book and said "It reads like The Good Food Guide!"*

Altogether, drinking was an integral part of working for alcohol companies and the ability to hold your own could be as important as research expertise. A director of Johnnie Walker (before it was taken over by Diageo) always had the drinks trolley arrive in his office on the dot of 12 noon and any agency visitor not partaking enthusiastically had their chances of another project severely reduced.

> • *The research manager of a leading beer company always turned up early at 9.30am to see the tasting session in which their beer was offered to members of the public invited in off the street. This session usually provided him with a couple of early morning pints before he wandered off to test the town's pubs for the rest of the day.*

However in later years the industry clearly sobered up. This may in part have been due to the influence of the Americans who began to look askance at any alcohol-fuelled lunches. Their sober demeanour was typified by a meeting with a management team from McDonald's involving a lecture by one of the UK's most lively leading statisticians, after which he tried to interest them in loosening up socially at a gathering in the bar of their hotel. But they would not lower their guard and he concluded that American corporate attitudes were stiffly unbending.

In qualitative research there are many stories of occasions in which the best of intentions are not fulfilled. As examples of the things which can go wrong ….

> • *The principal technique in automotive research is the car clinic in which a mock-up of a possible new model is appraised by potential customers. On one occasion, a 1986 Jaguar XJ6 was presented in the form of a clay model which cost up to £2million to construct. Unfortunately the research venue had to be changed at the last moment and a local sports centre was used instead. The heavy full-size model was put in position, followed by lengthy sickening cracking noise as the 'Jaguar' started to sink through a widening gap in the floor. The owner of the sports centre had neglected to say there was a swimming pool under his flimsy covering floor.*

> • *Another instance was a study for Kerrygold margarine, for which the client was required to deliver the product, specified in terms of its collective total weight. Unfortunately, the client weighed the Kerrygold complete with the heavy ice packaging it was boxed in. So the actual amount delivered was a fraction of the amount needed for the study.*

> • *And during the presentation of research on a leading well-known fragrance, the big client stood up, slammed his files onto the table and shouted, 'Don't give me all that psychological clap-trap', and stormed out.*

Any research buyer will want to avoid such problems and get the best out of their research suppliers. A very brief checklist of ways to choose and use them wisely might include:

- Prepare a written brief, and ensure your own management has a clear idea of what can and cannot be resolved by the research.
- Identify the supplier's level of previous experience in your field.
- Do they subscribe to the MRS Code of Conduct?
- Have they got sufficient resources (i.e. interviewers, executives) to do the job?
- Ensure a good working relationship. (Will you enjoy working with them?)
- Are you clear as to how much of the project will be delegated to junior staff?
- Have they given you full information on what parts of the project will be subcontracted to other organisations?
- If you change your mind about some aspect of the project, have you been clearly told the cost and timing implications?
- Have you discussed their findings and conclusions before they deliver them?

As the head of a research company said, "The client is not always right, but they need to be convinced of that sometimes." Giving them the bad news is always tricky, and some examples of that:

- *A particularly difficult client wanted a research company to recruit group participants for a study of dairy foods, according to strict criteria agreed with him. This was done very precisely but, viewing the assembled group from behind a one-way mirror, he asserted that they didn't look like his idea of his target market, and he departed unhappy. But their ethnicity, jobs, and purchase behaviour matched his recruitment criteria exactly.*

- *Similarly, when presenting the results of a study of owners' opinions of cat food, a young researcher said that one of the ways that owners judged cat food was whether it was thought firm, or sloppy. The client interjected strongly: "And what would you say if I told you there is no such thing as sloppy cat food?" Fortunately the head of the research agency restored credibility by saying: "Well you might believe that to be the case, but it is not what the consumers think."*

It was true in the past, as it is now, that not all of those commissioning research projects are familiar with the territory:

- *Way back, in 1963 a celebrity multimillionaire hairdresser known as 'TeasyWeasy Raymond' decided to stand for parliament and wanted to test his level of support in his chosen constituency.*

His attempts to join one of the two major parties had failed, as it did with the Liberals when they found he could not name their leader. So he said to hell with the parties, he was a celebrity and would run as an independent.

The poll he commissioned found his level of support against all the parties was negligible and awareness of him against other celebrities such David Frost the TV interviewer and Sir John Hunt the Everest climber was also negligible. Not one voter in the poll sample would vote for him against any other candidate.

It got worse: when asked what issues he hoped to run on he mentioned only one – the reform of the Jockey Club, with which he had had a recent disagreement. But sadly the poll found that this had no appeal, especially when compared with the economy, unemployment and all other issues.

However in the end, all was not in vain: the poll was worth the money he spent on it as it persuaded him that politics was not for him.

Three more examples of clients unwilling or unable to act upon the good advice delivered by the research:

> - *Following a study conducted for a long-established merchant bank, the researcher told them that its reputation among many potential customers was poor, and he had the temerity to quote one respondent who echoed others of the same mind, by saying the bank was run by "a load of useless toffee-nosed twits who couldn't run a whelk stall." While acknowledging the validity of the findings, his client decided to hide the report from his fellow directors, and unsurprisingly the bank had since been unable to keep pace with its competitors in this market and eventually went bust.*

> - *In similar vein, a research-based consultancy report submitted to a leading Fleet Street publishing house included a recommendation that the Managing Director should be replaced. Since that report was delivered initially to that MD, it is not surprising that he put it in a drawer in his desk and it never saw the light of day again.*

How can you possibly suggest that we're incompatible, Daphne, seeing that we're in the same socio-demographic grouping?

- *In 1966 the Daily Mail combined with the MCC (the governing body for English cricket) to commission a survey measuring interest in cricket at all levels. Presenting the results to the lordly Ted Dexter and other luminaries in the hallowed Long Room at Lord's cricket ground, it was explained (to no-one's surprise) that cricket was very popular at Test Match level and on village greens throughout the nation, but county cricket was not, partly because it was not played on Sundays nor in the evenings when those at work could actually attend. Despite the researchers' recommendations for change, county cricket matches remained poorly attended and it took the MCC (and the Law) more than 10 years to correct the identified deficiencies with innovations such as test matches on Sundays and 20-over evening matches.*

There's a C2 in reception to see you, sir.'

Reprinted by kind permission of the Evening Standard.

However research suppliers do not always view their research-buying clients so negatively, especially when international studies are involved:

> • *One young trainee recalled an alcohol-fuelled flight followed by a ride in a stretch limo to stay at the Waldorf Astoria Hotel New York, all paid for by their client.*

> • *Another project was for a leading British airline and involved some focus groups in New York. After their work had been completed, the researchers arrived very early at JFK for the return journey, and were offered an immediate flight home in a DC10, not the larger and grander 747 they had booked. This involved a lengthy stop-over in Manchester so, taking a risk, they said 'no thanks'. At which point the check-in person said "Ok if you don't mind staying overnight we'll book you in to a local hotel with a complimentary dinner, and then you can fly home tomorrow on Concorde." They didn't say 'no' to that idea.*

> • *Likewise, working for a drinks brand on a project concerning Madeira wine, the client invited the researchers to Madeira and Lisbon, with them assuming that they were to present the findings. They were wined and dined in the best places in Madeira, but found they were never actually called upon to deliver the presentation: it was simply a jolly at the client's expense.*

To provide a voice for the active buyers of research, The Association of Users of Research Agencies (AURA) was set up in 1965 and by 1986 it had 77 Member companies. But over the years many of these Research Managers have ceded their decision making powers to their Purchasing Departments, which have tended to impose a more bureaucratic Procurement Process: these will try ensure compliance with set standards but often seem less concerned about technical excellence than with choosing the lowest-cost supplier. As far back as 1982 this loss of influence among Research Managers was accompanied by increased familiarity with research across other management disciplines, as foreseen by one of the leading corporate research buyers who wrote:

> • *"The marketing executive is now well enough informed about research problem definition to be able to cut out the cumbersome and costly company research department and go to research suppliers direct. The company researcher is left at best a purchasing agent, and at worst redundant."*

In recent years this development has been facilitated by survey packages such as Survey Monkey, and research has now become a game which anyone can play.

Similarly, in advertising agencies the role of the researcher has been largely yielded to the Planners and Marketing Executives, who aim to take the research further into its applications in the marketplace.

> • *Among the many arguments as to why one should prefer one research supplier rather than another, the most original came on at least one occasion from a research supplier well known for his strong religious beliefs. To reinforce his sales pitch, he asserted that by the power of prayer he could ensure that the sampling errors in his company's surveys were less than those of his competitors.*

Qualitative Research

Despite the growth of quantitative research, much of it now based on massive databanks and electronic data collection, smaller-scale qualitative research conducted mostly through in-depth interviews, focus groups and observational studies, remains essential and widely used. In the UK this was led in the 1950s and later by the brilliance of Bill Schlackman, who had himself learned from Ernest Dichter, known in the USA as 'The Father of Motivational Research'. He was followed by a distinguished series of leaders in this field including Harry Henry, David Collins, Peter Cooper, Mary and John Goodyear, Wendy Gordon, Roy Langmaid, Judie Lannon and many others.

But there has always been a cultural division in the research industry between the qualitative and quantitative researchers, and arguments between them over the validity of their respective techniques have gone on for many years. The Quant specialists argued that on account of the very small samples covered by qualitative focus groups and in-depth interviews, claims to generate statistically representative results were spurious.

In 1979, a prominent research buyer asserted that there are "only rare occasions when qualitative research can be used without subsequent quantification. Then in 1981, the MRS Chairman wrote "…However enthusiastic they are about the product, two groups of eight housewives in Bolton cannot guarantee the success of the national launch of any product". This almost immediately brought forth a storm of protest from several leading qualitative researchers which the Chairman simply dismissed with "I never cease to be amazed by the sensitivity of some qualitative researchers …"

The Qualitative specialists counter such disdain by saying that Quant surveys mostly lack depth and insight into what people really think and do, and their own qualitative techniques provide essential insights into why particular behaviour patterns and opinions exist, and how they might be altered.

As examples of this, –

- *A focus group conducted among young mothers who had difficulty in breast-feeding their new-born babies revealed an unexpectedly high level of anxiety, coupled with low-self-esteem. As they shared their experiences together, several participants were reduced to tears and the focus group quickly turned into a therapy session, providing new insights to the client, a bottle feed manufacturer, who was thereby able to greatly improve the design of his product and advertising.*

- *After becoming more relaxed in each other's company and with the moderator, a group of hard-nosed secondhand car salesmen opened up in a way that would never have been possible in a quantitative survey. They readily admitted putting sand in carburettas and winding back mileometers (both illegal) to improve their business results.*

- *Sufferers from Bell's Palsy, which creates paralysis in face muscles, were recruited for a special focus group, and for the first time found an opportunity to share their experiences and worries, which provided valuable insights which less collaborative research techniques would never have identified.*

- *The man who invented Bailey's Irish Cream started by commissioning focus groups to test reactions to the idea and to the liquid he had devised. Watching from behind the mirror with others from the research company, he could see one participant after another saying how much they disliked the idea. But after a while they also noticed that the same participants not only finished their 'taster' glasses of Baileys, but kept asking for more. And the rest is history, with Baileys becoming the world's largest-selling liqueur.*

These projects epitomise the classic quote by advertising legend David Ogilvy: "Consumers don't think how they feel. They don't say what they think and don't do what they say." More recently, one leading research company CEO has said "Our job has moved on from stopping marketing from doing stupid things, to focusing on the promotion business with emotional measures that directly contribute to brand-building and marketing success: when people feel more, they buy more."

Of course the real solution for most clients is to use both, with the qual undertaken first and its findings being used to ensure the relevance of the questions asked in the quant stage which follows. Between the two main qualitative methods, **focus groups** usually serve best as a means of generating ideas about a service or product field, while **individual depth interviews** will identify the motivations and needs which drive people's choices.

> • *Another early example of how qualitative research can identify needs and behaviour while quantitative methods will not, is provided by the oft-repeated story from the 1960s of how the Polaroid Camera company was puzzled by its own success and needed to know why its main product was so popular. In-depth interviewing covered the question of where and why the camera was being used: this revealed, to the surprise of the company, that the prime location for using it and getting its instant prints was the bedroom, though it did not go further to identify the bedroom practices involved.*

Among the best stories of how interesting and informative contact with the public can be, are those which arise from the things which happen during the execution of qualitative research:

- *Setting up research on samples of a new food product, the convenor tried tasting them beforehand, thought them disgusting, but remembered to say nothing so her opinions did not influence reactions in the group sessions which followed. In the discussion groups, questions on the concept went down well, but when it was followed by the tasting everyone thought they were disgusting. Classic comment from one participant: "Now I understand why companies do market research." Mercifully, the client saw the funny side of this, cancelled the product, and sent the market development team back to the kitchens.*

- *Working on a research project on cosmetic breast enlargement, the interviewer had to travel via the Docklands Light Railway to 'Gallion's Reach' in order to interview an attractive young woman aged about 24 in her top floor flat. She was the single mother of a seven year old child with day job, and a more lucrative night job as a lap dancer, for which she had had her breasts enlarged. "You can feel them if you like", she said casually, stripping off her top. So that was the scene, with the interviewer cautiously feeling those breasts. As she said to her colleagues later "Qualitative research is a strange and wonderful job".*

- *The early impact of qualitative market research was also illustrated by focus groups conducted for a leading life insurance company. Its Chief Executive decided to sit in on one such session, unseen behind a one-way glass screen. Having seen the level of ignorance and incomprehension in reactions to his print advertisements he said afterwards "This has changed my whole working life. We have been producing ads to impress our competitors, not realising that they were not understood at all by our potential customers".*

- *The cultural distance between some clients and the public was also illustrated when one of the leading banks commissioned research to test reactions to a new charging system they wanted to introduce. Four options were presented, but it was found that none of them were understood by participating members of the public. And it was a struggle to get the bankers to face reality and agree to a simpler way of describing their options.*

- *A project undertaken for a leading brand of incontinence pads involved recruiting groups of men aged 75-85 suffering from mild to severe incontinence. Recruited from around Surrey, they had to be taken in a hired van to a viewing facility in central London. However they had to stop several times on the journey, using toilets in hotels they passed en route. In this way, the 2-hour focus group took 6-7 hours to complete: many stops, many loo's, but thankfully no accidents. This project earned the unkindly name 'Project Sprinkle'.*

And although they do not happen often, there are some mishaps to avoid:

- *On a hot, humid midsummer day in the Kingston on Thames marketplace, a taste test on Christmas chocolates being launched by a liqueur brand was undertaken. But the chocolates were melting so fast, running down the table top and mixing up the flavours. Lesson learned: don't test Christmas chocs in midsummer without some way of keeping them cool.*

> • *A research project was being held in a hotel room, the recruited participants being young men. As they arrived, they signed in, and were given a drink and the money they had been promised for attending. Half an hour into the discussion one of them asked to go to the loo. Then another did so, followed soon by another, and another. They never reappeared, so the convenor ended up with a nearly empty room. Lesson for the future: give them their money after completion of the session.*

> • *On another occasion, when sitting with the client behind a one-way mirror in an adjoining room in order to watch focus group participants unseen by them, the researcher had to restrain him physically: he was losing his temper with a participant who was criticising his product and he was determined to go charging into the group to correct the supposedly misinformed comments he was hearing.*

Often such scenes are fuelled by alcohol consumption and eventually a Golden Rule was established by leading research companies that 'Alcohol is our enemy, even when it is the Client'. And one must not serve too much (or any) alcohol in groups, even if such drinks are being tested. This rule was prompted by scenes such as:

> • *The participant who had already had a few before arriving. He ended up by grabbing the moderator's advertising board, punching a hole in it, and standing in front of the viewing mirror shouting "this is all a load of **** crap".*

- *For a project about beer, someone thought it would be a good idea to conduct the focus groups in pubs. But in one group, two participants disagreed violently and started fisticuffs in the middle of the floor, until eventually the other participants threw them out onto the street.*

- *Testing two new bottled lagers in an 'A/B sip test' the client suddenly thought people would need more than a sip to test their beers properly. When this idea was enacted with full bottles and four more blank-labelled beers were added to the test, the word got around and a long queue formed of those wanting to take part. Soon enough, a raucous party got going, with the tables covered in bottles while the moderator tried to restore order with her sequence of questions:*

  "Which was better, A or B?"
  - *"Me myshelf, I prefer FFFFF"*
  - *"Yeahhh! FFFF is the best!"*
  - *"F is gooder I'm, telling you. Makes you feel fine"*
  - *"D is the star, definitely"*

  "Do you remember tasting A and B?"
  - *"Yes, we liked those, both of them"*
  - *"I preferred B. So I had three of those. No, wait, maybe it was A ...."*

What also emerges from such contact with the general public is their occasional tendency to hold strange beliefs about the world around them:

- o "Have you noticed ...(Brand X) have been refitting their stores with narrower entrances, so fat people can't get in?"
- o "Their (fast food chain) cows are bred in Argentina to be absolutely huge and barrel-shaped, to make it easier for them to turn them into burgers."

o "There's no actual milk in milkshakes."
o "I have heard that cows, before they were domesticated, used to hunt in packs, like dogs."

A special category of focus group participant is that of members of the medical profession. They are almost alone in demanding a substantial fee for doing so. Of course, the clients of much of this kind of research are the big pharmaceutical companies, and the medics may be justified in saying" Why should I help these highly profitable companies for free?"

> - *One example of this kind of research was a study on how they diagnosed and treated angina. Focus groups were held in a hotel near Heathrow, and it was hoped that some kind of consensus would emerge. However instead they chose to disagree vehemently, even on the initial stages of treatment, some advocating immediate bed rest and others urging their patients to exercise rigorously, one of them advocating "One good pant a week."*
>
> *So no consensus, and at the end of the evening they all jumped into their Jaguars and drove themselves home.*

To help ensure they did not take themselves too seriously, one leading qualitative researcher lightened the tone of the argument and took a rise out of the reports produced by his own colleagues and competitors by offering a list of typical comments on research findings, and their hidden meanings:

"While it would perhaps be dangerous to generalise from six group discussions..." *What you read here should be taken with a pinch of salt*

"It has long been known ..." *I didn't look up the original reference*

"It is believed that ..." *I think*

"It is generally believed that ..."   *A couple of my colleagues think so too*

"Three of the respondents made interesting comments ..."   *The comments of the others don't fit my story.*

In 1973 there was considerable correspondence in the MRS Newsletter on the subject of group discussions (not yet called focus groups) which generated a great deal of heat. This was prompted initially by a leading research buyer who noted that "we are experiencing a boom in which corners are being cut ... Consequently we now hear continuing complaints about professional group-goers, non-smokers in groups of smokers, etc. ... Obviously control by the MRS would not be easy, but I believe it is vital ... to restore order in what is becoming a veritable jungle of the good, the bad and the downright dishonest."

This problem was highlighted for several years, by stories of professional group-goers in Buckhurst Hill in Essex, and in Winchester. One can only hope that it no longer happens, though this recent story does suggest it may not have been eradicated entirely:

> • *Participants should be recruited independently without collusion, but in one recent group a participant gave the game away. He expressed annoyance at the start when, to make everyone feel at ease, the convenor asked them to introduce themselves and tell a bit about themselves: "Bloody stupid games! We all know each other, can't we just say our names?"*

Quantitative Research

On account of the larger numbers involved, the greater proportion of the national spend on marketing and social research has consisted in quantitative surveys, in which certainty in proportions, estimates and decisions is sought.

As indicated earlier, many such surveys are designed to explore particular products or services and their place in their markets. Some are for testing new concepts, but as the research industry has matured an increasing proportion are not one-off studies, but are repeated or continuous, or are simply the mining of existing data sets for fresh insights. The biggest proportion of market research spend in the UK is on panel research, measuring market size, sales or media consumption such as TV audience behaviour.

The two biggest companies in the UK are Kantar (previously TNS Sofres and before that AGB) and Neilsen who carry out panel research ie continuous measurement of people's purchasing behaviour, and not contacting a fresh sample at each wave. One of the best known in the UK is Superpanel which began in 1990 and replaced previous large panel surveys carried out by AGB. To these should be added JICTAR which measures the size and composition of television audiences. Data were originally collected by postal surveys, then face to face, and finally it was (and still is) collected via barcodes and submitted every day electronically.

Among the repeat studies which collect information from fresh samples at each wave, either annually or more often, the most prominent are The Target Group Index (TGI), The National Food Survey, the Social Trends Survey, the annual GB Tourism Survey, and the National Readership Survey (JICNARS). In addition to these, there are the many business-to-business surveys, syndicated surveys of bank customers, both retail and corporate, travellers by train and bus, and similar surveys among hotel customers.

Both panel and fresh-sample repeated survey methods are essential for monitoring changes over time and, within that, most have to be very accurate not least because they are used to determine the advertising revenue of various media or the continuation of vital franchises (such as those enjoyed by the rail companies).

*Are you quite sure you switched off the Research company's
TV Household Usage Monitoring Eye?*

Surveys which are not constrained by the need for a high level of accuracy have greatly increased over the years, driven by the very low costs made possible through sampling via the internet and various databases which have been assembled. Forty years ago a leading Field Manager expressed concern over the decline in major survey response rates: in the decade 1965 to 1974, the National Readership Survey was based on a response rate which declined from 78% to 74%. In the National Food Survey it went down from 55% to 52%, in the National Travel Survey down from 80% to 70%, and in Greater London Council Surveys down from 79% to 73%. But now, as many surveys are internet-based and achieve less than 10%, things have got very much worse: a lot of work needs to be done to correct problems in sampling, and not all weighting may be adequate.

"Good afternoon—my company is conducting a survey in this area . . ."

Reproduced by permission of Punch

From the earliest days of the research business young executives were nearly always taught to pre-test the viability of quantitative survey questionnaires with a pilot survey in which maybe not more than a dozen interviews were completed in order to refine the wording or structure before being inflicted on the main survey sample. Under the pressures of modern delivery deadlines this happens too rarely nowadays.

> • *There are some legendary tales arising from the failure to pre-test: in its early days the multi-faceted Target Group Index was based on a long self-completion questionnaire left with a particular individual in each household, and it produced results which, grossed up, indicated that there are thousands of rugby players who wear ladies' knickers and brassieres. Clearly its questions were required to be answered by men, some of whom left the questionnaire lying around the house to be picked up and completed by their wives in an idle moment.*

- *The same nationwide survey found twice as many women as men answering 'Yes' to the question "Are you engaged to be married?" which suggested there were thousands of over-optimistic women across the nation.*

- *Sometimes the lack of pre-testing related to the product being asked about, rather than the research being undertaken: one type of aerosol could be activated by an instruction on the can to "Push up bottom". More than one respondent, asked to try using it, complained they found that anatomically difficult.*

Data Processing: One essential corner of the quantitative survey process is masterminded by the data processing specialists. Until the end of the 1950s questionnaires were analysed manually by clerical labour. Responses to questions were hand-counted using 'five-bar gates' as the basic counting unit. The research executive then percentaged them, some using a flat ruler-type slide rule and others a cylindrical one known to Americans as 'slip sticks'.

Later on, using computers, the DP department could apply corrective weighting, and deliver your results analysed in any way wanted, and it can be simultaneously connected to the data collection process.

Choosing and defining the weighting cells must be done carefully, so that final results are delivered which do not excessively reduce the effective sample size. An early example of what can go wrong was the Businessman's Readership Survey of 1968, in which one cell consisting of three interviews was, after weighting, grossed up to represent about five hundred. Thankfully the IPA Appraisals Committee, which evaluated the respectability of all print media research, was able to show that this survey needed to go back to the drawing board and be reworked before being released for use in media planning by advertisers and advertising agencies.

In recent years the research industry has discovered that by analysing large databanks containing product buying information the targeting of marketing activity can be much more precise. Similarly the use of internet surveys for sample surveys is so inexpensive and instantaneous that one is tempted to overlook the very low response rates (usually less than 10%) which no amount of weighting can reliably correct. In 2018, a speaker at an evening meeting at the Institute of Practitioners in Advertising was inclined to say "Big Data is like teenage sex: it claims to know how to do it, and claims to do it, but actually doesn't."

Statistical Uncertainties: This is not the place to set out the statistical theories, sampling procedures and assessments of likely error which much survey research is based on. Few surveys in which accurate measurement is needed are based on less than 400 interviews. Most opinion polls need to be based on 1,000+ interviews to measure party percentage levels which are often similar to one another, and the big syndicated panels are usually based on 10,000 or more, so that the supposed margin of error on any reported percentage can be said to be less than 3%.

> • *In the early days, some clients supposed that a massive number of interviews was needed to achieve accuracy. In a 1959 survey on attitudes to the re-nationalisation of steel, the client asked for a million interviews, of which 248,000 were actually completed.*

But it should be added that *anything* based on a sample cannot pretend to 100% accuracy. This fact can be particularly upsetting to a roomful of accountants, as they are professionally trained to be mistrustful of any such notion. Confronted with a table of figures perhaps adding to 99% or 101% on account of rounding, and anyway subject to sampling error, they will immediately wish to reject it as 'unaudited' and therefore unacceptable. The cultural difference is that while survey researchers are careful to define each item on any such table, but recognise that their results must be subject to sampling error, accountants are used to creating balance sheets in which the figures are precise, but the definitions of each item may be less so.

> • *A universal research truism which should be more widely known and accepted is that promulgated through 'Twyman's Law', named after the late Tony Twyman, one of the Directors of the Research Bureau. His everlasting claim to fame derives from his rule that "the more surprising a finding from any survey is, the more likely that it is the result of some error in sampling, questioning, analysis or interpretation".*

Any newcomer to survey research need not be put off by a supposed requirement to know statistical theory and practice in detail. In 1973 readers of the MRS Newsletter were invited to test their statistical expertise by finding the odd one out in each of these categories:

Q1. Arithmetic mean, variance, mode, median.
Q2. Pie chart, ogive, histogram, moving average.
Q3. Factor Analysis, Kelly Grids, Canonical Analysis, AID.
Q4. Chi-square, t-test, null hypothesis, Kolmogorov-Smirnov two-sample test.
Q5. Simple random sample, random numbers, random route, quota sample.

(Correct answers are: Q1, variance; Q2, moving average; Q3, Kelly Grids; Q4, null hypothesis; Q5, random numbers)

Few readers were able to identify the correct answers, leading to a conclusion that once you have absorbed the basic principles of statistics it is a form of knowledge you do not need to know precisely as long as you know where to look it up.

"Frankly, Harold, you're beginning to bore everyone with your statistics."

And to reassure those who are still uneasy about sampling matters here is a story told about the late Philip Mitchell of the British Market Research Bureau when he was working in Dublin:

- *"He encountered a client complaining about the sample size of the Republic of Ireland Target Group Index (TGI) being too small (it was 2,500). At that point Philip pulled out of his back pocket a map of Dublin, unfolded it on the table and said to the client "Would you trust this map to lead you around Dublin?" The client said "Yes, absolutely", at which point Philip said "The scale of this map is 1:1000, which is exactly the same ratio as the TGI sample size is to the population of Ireland". The client at that point had nowhere to go!"*

Finally, one should not suppose that the statisticians across the research industry were dry-as-dust pointy-heads. In 1974, a report on a statistics course held in Cambridge described it as follows:

> • *"With an even mix of genders attending the course, social activities were not lacking. On one evening the local disco was patronised, but the social highlight occurred on another night, which entailed a long evening of drinking and singing at one of the Cambridge pubs, whose landlord was a friend of one of the delegates."*

"Do you come here often/occasionally/infrequently/never?"

Reproduced by permission of the Evening Standard.

Sophisticated Analyses: The ultimate aim of many market research surveys is to provide a means of identifying the most likely targets for their products or services. Early on, it was called market segmentation, and it sometimes developed into a modelling process whereby the computer could identify various groups, each with distinct characteristics. Then in the more mature markets, where an increased number of competitors were all striving for market share, there came a need to identify the issues on which a competitor could most advantageously differentiate itself from others purporting to deliver the same product or service:

- *To compete against the dominance of Mars in the petfood market, Spillers commissioned qual and quant research which identified three owner-animal archetypes as shown in these three cartoons by Rex Audley – Owners, Spoiling Parents and Companions:*

Owners   *Spoiling Parents*   *Companions*

Of these, the last had been largely ignored by the leading brands and this provided Spillers with marketplace success following the launch of their Spillers' Goodlife product, based on dogs which had a strong companionable role.

> • *One of the principal products of a leading manufacturer of bathroom accessories was toilet paper, and a definitive segmentation study undertaken for them apparently divided the human race into two distinct segments – the 'Folders' and the 'Scrunchers'. (Another such research project identified a third category, of 'Wrappers', who fold the paper around the hand to avoid the trauma of 'Finger Push-through').*
>
> *Later, the company's enthusiastic Research Manager asked his research suppliers to set up a quantitative panel of about 400 toilet paper users who were provided with diaries in order to record how many sheets were used on each occasion, and folded how many times. When it was suggested to him that people were unlikely to be willing or to remember to do that each time, he said "Don't worry, to remind them we have invented a toilet roll holder with a bell on it, which will loudly go 'Ping' every time it is used". With visions of neighbours complaining 'There they go again', the researchers declined to do the project.*

These sophisticated needs were met by a range of statistical products with names such as Factor Analysis, Conjoint Analysis, Multiple Regression, the Kelly Repertory Grid, the St James Model, Data Fusion and Geodemographics.

> • *In the 1980s, the last of these was used in a segmentation study combining Big Data from the TGI with geodemographic mapping techniques to identify what became known as 'The Dinner Party Set': they accounted for only 8% of the adult population, but 49% of the gin market, 44% of the scotch market and 29% of the wine market. Twenty five years later, the children of this segment were in the vanguard of the renaissance of gin as a popular drink.*

Other worthwhile procedures included the battery of attitude questions known as Likert Scales, but Martin Fishbein, Professor of Social Psychology at the LSE, warned that these on their own would not be predictive because you also need to ask how strongly beliefs are held and whether positive or negative feelings were held on the matter in hand.

> • *In 1963 these types of analysis were described in a verse penned by a leading researcher and published in the journal 'Applied Statistics':*
>
> *'If you want to deal best with your questions,*
> *Use multiple regression techniques;*
> *A computer can do in a minute*
> *What otherwise done, would take weeks.*
> *For 'predictor selection' procedures*
> *Will pick just the ones best for you,*
> *And provide the best-fitting equation*
> *For the data you've fitted it to.'*

> • *However, some prominent researchers continued to view these clever methods with a degree of scepticism. Professor Ehrenberg described as his greatest 'bête noir' a process he called 'Sonking' – the Scientification of Non-Knowledge. He added "That is, the practice of dressing up some theory or model to see if it 'fitted'. Not surprisingly, rigorous analysis almost always shows it didn't."*

Advertising Research

One very important category of research is that commissioned by advertising agencies and their advertisers, and in the UK this has been especially so since the birth of ITV. Although some of the most creative projects are of this kind, one should always be on guard against studies which are commissioned by the agencies simply to justify their advertising plans.

Advertising research is often viewed with apprehension by the creative departments, keen that their creative work should not be rubbished by it. In 1978, the creative director of a leading US ad agency went so far as to address the annual convention of the American Research Association as follows:

"Research is a crutch for people unwilling or unable to make decisions .... There is no way anyone can prejudge good creative work in a half-finished form, as it is in copy tests. Research robs advertising of its most effective force – human judgment."

Against that, David Ogilvy, founder of the Ogilvy and Mather agency, previously declared in 1962 that "Advertising people who ignore research are as dangerous as generals who ignore decodes of enemy signals."

And he put forward rules for research users and practitioners, of which the most significant were:

- Money spent on market research before the creative people get on with their job is worth twice the value of money spent afterwards

"Tell us, what exactly do you look for in a fish finger?"

- The most important role of the market researcher is to offer creative insights into problems
- Always separate reactions to the advertising from reactions to the product
- Filter out the emotional from the rational in creative market research
- Never give a research de-brief unless the creative people are present

One example of the way in which research can ensure that mistaken advertising communication strategies are improved or abandoned, lay in a project designed to test reactions to a new chocolate bar called a 'Logger':

- *It was intended to be a competitor to the well-established 'Yorkie' bar and the advertising for it was based on the Monty Python ditty 'I'm a lumberjack and I'm ok'. However the research soon found that especially in the north of England the word 'log' had unfortunate lavatorial associations, as in 'Drop a log'. But despite all that the research told them, the client insisted on launching the 'Logger' together with its advertising campaign, – only for it to sink without trace.*

Early in the 21st Century, it became evident that advertising people needed to be told how different their own lifestyles and perceptions were from those of ordinary people:

- *A study conducted in 2016 by Thinkbox among 'ad people' showed they spent 24% of their time watching TV on non-TV devices, and they thought 37% of the general public did the same. However the real proportion, derived from a nationwide survey of the public, was just 2%: holding up a mirror to the industry it showed how different the lifestyles of ad people are in their working hours, leisure time, device ownership, media subscriptions and social media use.*

Newspapers and Other Media

Among the most active users of market research are the media owners who need to know what their viewers, listeners or readers think and do, and in particular to demonstrate to advertisers how many of them are seeing or hearing the advertisements they carry. They are also the principal means whereby the results of public opinion polls are conveyed to the public.

In a speech given in 1972 a leading advertising mogul made a scathing attack on UK print media research, saying (i) it arrives too late, (ii) its demographic definitions are hopelessly out of date, (iii) readership figures for monthly magazines are a nonsense, (iv) the techniques for measuring readership of small-circulation up-scale publications lack relevance, (v) the data are useless to media men in practical terms, etc. But he concluded that "we are poor media researchers but, comparing with the rest of the world, unfortunately I do not know where to find better."

Much of that is no longer true, but then he also offered this tongue-in-cheek guidance to aspiring new entrants to media research (much of which does hold true today):

1. Never say yes or no.
2. Do keep your jargon up to date.
3. Try to get your name attached to something specific in this business – ie 'the Farnes-Barnes Method' or 'the Heathcliffe Histogram' etc. This is the way your name will be made.
4. Do write incomprehensible articles for publications media men are supposed to read, but don't.
5. Do not use simple words when difficult ones are there for you, ie not 'bar chart' but rather 'histogram'.
6. Invent your own phrases with a fine ring to them, i.e. 'point of oblivion', 'polychromatic function,' etc.
7. Do remember a graph can show anything you want, if you adapt the scale appropriately.

For advertising media research to be credible, it needs to be able to withstand technical appraisals by a panel of independent advertisers. For that reason it is often regarded as being among the most technically sound kinds of survey research.

This has not always been easy to achieve:

> • *In the late 1960s, at the time of the Pirate Radio Stations, researchers were commissioned to undertake a Scottish Radio Audience Survey for one of the offshore stations, Radio Scotland. The previous prison record of its owner should have provided a warning, and when the results were delivered showing that 48% of adults in Scotland had listened to Radio Scotland in the previous week, a positive response from the client was expected. But he refused to believe it, saying "<u>Everybody</u> in Scotland listens to our station," and he wouldn't pay for the survey. So he had to be taken to court, and it was then discovered that during the three-week interviewing period they had moved their ship from near Edinburgh, up north around Cape Wrath with its signal getting fainter and fainter, before anchoring in the Clyde near Glasgow with its larger population. The case was won in the end, but it took time and a lot of argument.*

Later, in New York, the assumption from UK experience that all such media studies were conducted objectively were shown to be false. It was widely assumed among research suppliers in the USA that they were mostly bent in the directions required by the radio stations commissioning them.

Back in 1970, market research on editorial content can claim to have helped to save the fledgling career of Jilly Cooper, at a time when it was under threat:

> • *Harry Evans, Editor of the Sunday Times, was under
> severe pressure from colleagues to get rid of this eccentric
> and talkative lady so they could concentrate on their more
> serious journalism. Hoping to find evidence to justify
> letting her go, he asked to see the results of the research
> department's weekly survey among readers. However this
> showed that both men and women in large numbers were
> finding their way to Jilly's column in the Women's Section,
> and it was one of the most widely read in the whole paper.
> Armed with this evidence, Harry could not justify sacking
> her, and this paved the way for her lifetime role of adding
> to the gaiety of the nation.*

But despite all attempts to justify the research process, one should always be wary of its shortcomings:

> • *An article in Cosmopolitan Magazine urged us not to take
> market research too seriously, instancing a survey of
> shoppers in which 92% claimed to have read at least two
> issues of a publication called 'Supermarket Age'— which
> does not in fact exist.*

Political Polling

Even though political opinion polls constitute only about 3% of the business of the market research industry, their impact on public consciousness is immense, especially when they fail, as they occasionally do, to predict election results. The pressure to achieve accuracy is, if anything, greater than is the case with any other kind of survey research, with only the last-minute exit poll maintaining an unerring reputation for predictive reliability.

Although most politicians nowadays understand their value and limitations, in the early days some prominent political figures were not afraid to parade their disbelief. In 1973, Michael Foot, later leader of the Labour Party, was widely quoted as saying "I have always regarded public opinion polls, audience ratings, and a sizeable chunk of what passes under the name of market research as tosh, and dangerous tosh at that". And Richard Crossman, whilst editing the New Statesman, said "I am only convinced of the findings of a Gallup Poll when they confirm my own impression of what the public is thinking".

However, in an address to the Market Research Society Annual Conference in 1970, the Minister for Technology, the Right Honourable Anthony Wedgwood Benn, dispelled the myth of market researchers as the Hidden Persuaders helping to dupe a guileless public, in saying "The market researcher forms a valuable communication link between the citizen and the advertiser".

'In case you're interested, your approval rating around here has slipped to a scant 23%.'

In the early days of political polling, the relationship between the polls and the press was not easy. In 1974 the head of a leading polling company wrote:

> • *"One of the most problematic features of opinion polling is the treatment of polling by the press. There is a love-hate relationship between the few journalists who understand them and the remainder who dislike them. The polls have deprived both journalists and politicians of the unchallenged ability to speak for public opinion."* For instance, no longer could they walk into a pub in a town where a by-election was taking place and claim to have sounded out local opinion reliably.

Following the 1974 General Election, there was a great deal of argument about the accuracy of opinion polls and their impact on the reputation of market research, and this has continued ever since. Back then, there were stories of clients cancelling projects already commissioned. For instance a leading qualitative research company reported that a client had cancelled a product test already commissioned. Nothing wrong with the methodology; no criticisms of the questionnaire; the cost was acceptable. But the client asked "Why should we spend money on research when it can't come up with the right answer?"

But a more measured response came from the Lord Leverhulme, Chairman of Lever Bros, who commented "If this makes my competitors give up market research, I will be very happy".

> • *In determining which poll subjects should be covered for a national newspaper, the pollster and the editor need to be impartial, ethically sound and willing to present all sides of an argument. In the 1970s the Editor of the Daily Express repeatedly asked for yet another poll on hanging, as he well knew that around 84% of the public backed hanging, as did he. The polling company had to say 'no'. But many years later another leading polling company caved in to similarly repeated requests from another leading newspaper. When it was suggested that they should desist, the pollster replied that they couldn't say 'no' to these repeated surveys on hanging because "it would endanger the earnings we gain from the editorial and advertising research we also do for them".*

Such agenda-setting polls must be guarded against, and the same goes for the kind of agree-disagree batteries of questions often used. If they do not cover the issues reflecting both sides of the argument, they can only be regarded as biased.

In the early days of the opinion polls there was bitter rivalry between the leading polling organisations on these and other issues:

> • *NOP believed in clustered random sampling from the electoral registers, while Gallup preferred to base their surveys on searching for correct quotas of young, old, male, female etc respondents in each location. Moderating the bitter 'Quota versus Random' argument between Henry Durant of Gallup and Mick Shields of NOP on TV's Tonight programme, the interviewer invited them to resolve their differences over a friendly lunch together. Henry's tart response was "Well, he can bring his sandwiches to my office if he wants to".*

Though such a body did not exist during several general elections in the past, nowadays the British Polling Council exists to keep the peace, guard against such errors and reveal the shortcomings of biased or technically inadequate polls.

But it remains true that, as Nils Bohr, Nobel Prize Winning Physicist, said: "Prediction is difficult, especially about the future."

- *The mischief which journalists sometimes inflict on researchers became apparent when the 'Tonight' TV journalist Michael Barratt asked to accompany an interviewer as she pounded the streets administering her by-election survey questionnaire. Having spent the morning doing that, he 'borrowed' the questionnaire and re-visited an old lady in order to find her rather confused answers on economic and defence issues to be different from those originally given to the interviewer. That gave him a juicy story for his programme that night, emphasising that the polling was not reliable. Another view might be that it was instead a much-needed demonstration that ordinary voters are much less interested and knowledgeable about political issues than Westminster likes to assume.*

4. OUT IN THE WIDER WORLD

Conferences and Seminars

Many of the most important technical advances in market research are aired at the various conferences and seminars throughout each year.

The Annual Conference of the Market Research Society is the most important of these. It is usually attended by up to 1,000 research practitioners in Brighton or some other suitable resort, or more recently in London. One report from the 1980s described how the need to relax and get away from day-to-day problems was facilitated at the opening cocktail party by "copious amounts of alcohol from the free bar." And the cliquey nature of these occasions was highlighted by a report that while younger delegates worried "My God, I know hardly anyone here" the older delegates looked equally worried and were saying "My God, I know nearly everyone here."

> • *In May 1978, this report on the Brighton Conference: "If readers or participants at last month's 21st Annual Conference have any doubts that this was the best, the best attended, the best organised, and the Conference by which they will all be judged in future, then all doubts must be dispelled. The results of the work that the Conference Sub-Committee produced could hardly be faulted, and for its Chairman (who worked for British Gas) it was a personal triumph."*

- *However this report also noted that, "after an exciting pulsating evening with loads of drink, dancing and fun, late into the hours of Friday night two researchers of variable sex, differing social class, but the same age group, were to be seen travelling incessantly up and down in the lift, clutching blindly at one another .... "*

- *And a Danish commentator attending the Conference in 1984 reported that "apart from the Royal Pavilion, Brighton does not have many cultural attractions. Brilliant restaurants exist but they are few in number, and the hotels are not outstanding with the exception of The Grand ... Brighton can in no way compete with Monte Carlo, Vienna, Geneva, Amsterdam or other cities where market research Congresses are held. But the MRS Conferences have something special – the atmosphere, which I can best describe as warm, friendly and relaxed."*

In the early days of research, many Conference presentations were very poorly prepared and delivered, sometimes hand-written on acetates and shown via an overhead projector, and all too often the credibility of the speaker was diminished. And the same held true away from the Conference, of presentations of project results to clients. In 1975, the MRS Chairman wrote "It has always seemed strange to me that in a business like ours which depends on good clear communication either in the written word or in a visual form, the standard of presentation seen at many of our conferences has rarely been more than tolerably good and is often appallingly bad".

> • One example of such a disaster occurred at the MRS
> Annual Conference in 1984 during delivery of a paper by
> a speaker deploring the current lack of presentation skills
> across the industry. In a packed hall, the audience clearly
> hoped for a come-uppance, and midway through his
> session the speaker was confounded by an overheating
> slide projector which a conference technician at the back
> of the hall tried to alleviate by lifting and fanning its
> underside. He continued undeterred, with the slides slowly
> rising up the wall and tracking their way back across the
> ceiling, causing increasing hilarity among the audience.
> He carried on regardless, claiming that this was "simply
> a deliberate demonstration of how to manage unexpected
> presentational problems." But he was finally undone when
> he walked off the stage forgetting to remove the
> microphone around his neck, which nearly strangled him.

But in contrast to that, some conference presentations were much
more lively and well-delivered:

> • A paper delivered in Brighton was fittingly entitled
> 'Research to Help Plan the Future of a Seaside Resort'.
> The speaker rose at the start of his session to the loud
> music accompaniment of "I do Like to be Beside the
> Seaside" and on the screen was a set of six photographs
> of scantily clad models in bathing costumes. He then
> explained "The overture was played by Reginald Dixon
> on the organ of the Tower Ballroom Blackpool and the
> pictures were from the months Jan to June in a Pirelli
> calendar. For those who stay awake until the end of this
> paper, the finale will comprise the photos from July to
> December."

Especially in the 1980s, these occasions were also enlivened by
some famous entertainers and musicians attending its Grand Ball
such as (in 1980) Pan's People and the Band of the Royal Marines

counter marching across the floor (they also participated in 1983). In 1981 it featured the multi-talented Roy Castle, and Jeannette Charles whose act entailed her impersonating the Queen.

Earlier, in 1978 a cabaret provided by a group of well-known researchers from Ogilvy & Mather advertising agency, collectively known as 'The Red Braces' was a highlight of one evening, with verses sung to the tune of Gilbert and Sullivan's 'A Policeman's Lot Is Not A Happy One'. Two verses from this illustrate the life in research and in the Conference itself:

'When the field force isn't cheating on its mileage
Or demanding extra fees if there's a snag
Their capacity for fluffing awkward questions
Means questionnaire design is quite a drag.
They keep recruiting samples out of quota
'Cos interviewing neighbours is more fun,
With group discussions full of bum respondents –
A researcher's life is not a happy one.

When the conference time comes round again at Brighton,
And wine like water flows in every bar
The Agencies are free with gin and tonic
And each one tries to beat the rest by far,
All liquor we with eager swallows guzzle
As soon as every party has begun
And when you're lying underneath the table –
A researcher's life is not a happy one.

Other Conference happenings, mostly from the 1980s:

- *Charitable sweepstakes provided significant prizes, on one occasion including a Sinclair C5 vehicle, which was later seen cruising the hotel corridors. A group of delegates took it outside to test drive it on the promenade. Unfortunately they got too near the edge and it fell eight feet down onto the beach below. It then took them several hours into the night to retrieve it and clean it up. And incidentally the same lively group had earlier been seen cheering the tug of war between qualitative and quantitative delegates which had been organised.*

- *An eccentric independent research company chief made a habit of booking the best suite in the Grand Hotel, with a balcony directly above the entrance. Late night socialising was the focal point of the Conferences in those days. In one year, a group of regular visitors to his suite cornered the local market for flour, in order to make flour bombs on the night of the Conference Ball. Some excellent direct hits were scored on carefully selected delegates as they entered in evening dress below.*

- *A regular presence at the Annual Conference in those years was a leading statistician with a convivial and thirsty reputation. Returning from an extended drinking session with friends in a town pub he drove back to the Conference hotel in his car. Unfortunately, he was stopped by a policeman, obviously aware of Conference antics, who looked through the driver's window and, seeing his conference identity badge, simply asked "Are you having a good Conference then Tom?" – and let him go with a brief warning. It would not happen now.*

- *Such was the keenness to secure tickets to the Conference Ball that a group who had previously failed to obtain them before the box office was closed, disguised themselves as waiters and hired uniforms by bribing some hotel staff. They were surprisingly unnoticed by many of the diners and dispensed drinks freely to all their friends. However their service quickly deteriorated as their drink orders were mixed up. There were some heated exchanges, but most of the diners still failed to recognise these interloping amateurs in their waiter guise.*

- *At the Brighton Conference a prominent and well-heeled research company chief had a penchant for demonstrating the attributes of his super cars to impressionable young female researchers. As he headed off to a local beauty spot with one of them in the front seat next to him, his 'friends' decided to clip his wings by reporting to the police that his was a stolen car.*

Meanwhile, although there was strong interest in the intellectual sparring matches taking place in the main conference hall, it seems that some delegates used the occasion for social interaction of a more permissive kind:

- *One lady executive at the conference was reported as describing her efforts to repel the unwanted advances of an older and richer member of the opposite sex by saying "When I finally said 'No' he replied "Oh go on Suzie, you won't even notice it".*

At the Annual Conference in 1974, Action Research Ltd set up a Limerick Competition for delegates, the winner being a delegate from General Foods:

'At Bournemouth, a delegate faction
Suffered conference-paper reaction.
They resorted to jars
In casinos and bars
And solving limericks for Action.'

It should not be supposed however that all this frivolity obliterated the serious purposes of these annual conferences. The few early examples shown below were among the intellectually creative and demanding landmark papers delivered by distinguished speakers no longer with us:

1963: 'Research on Question Design' by Dr W A Belson, of the LSE.

1967: 'The Application of Repertory Grid Techniques to Problems in Market Research' by R L Braine of AGB Surveys and W A K Frost of Advertising Assessment Ltd.

1967: 'Can Research Evaluate the Creative Content of Advertising?' by Stephen King, of J Walter Thompson.

1970: 'The Role of Market Research in the Community' by Anthony Wedgwood Benn, MP.

1971: 'The Use of Market Research in Preventing Automobile Accidents' by Dr M Perry, of The Hebrew University.

1971: 'Causal Factors in the Development of Juvenile Stealing' by Dr W A Belson, of the LSE.

Later, when the 50th Anniversary of the founding of the Market Research Society was being celebrated in 1996, a report on the Conference over the previous 50 years called 'Milestones in Market Research', listed some key the papers from past conferences, which any younger researcher would still benefit from reading today:

- 'Sampling Errors in Practice' by Tom Corlett'
- 'The Use of Consumer Panels for Brand-share Prediction' by John Parfitt and B.J.K. Collins
- 'The Utility of the Classification of Residential Households' by Ken Baker, John Bermingham and Colin McDonald
- 'How do Consumers Feel Advertising Works?' by Wendy Gordon
- 'Sensitivity Panels: the Use of Trained Respondents in Qualitative Research' by William Schlackman
- 'How do you Like Your Data: Raw, Al Dente or Stewed?' by Tim Bowles and Bill Blyth
- 'Data Fusion: An Appraisal and Experimental Evaluation' by Ken Baker, Paul Harris and John O'Brien

> - *Similarly taking things seriously, at the MRS Conferences throughout the 1970s and 1980s a man called Michael Stewart, an economist and econometrician, would always sit in the front row clutching his book of papers, and at question time after any paper had been delivered he would be first on his feet. He would glare at the speakers and then aggressively attack their arguments in some specific way, starting with, for example, "I am astonished you could address this topic without referring to the works of X and Y, and you clearly have not read the works of Z ...." The speakers were left aghast and unable to respond well.*

This may be an extreme example, but it illustrates the fastidiousness of the critiques made of the papers delivered at the Conference during these years, and the controversies which enlivened each session in a way that perhaps happens less fully nowadays.

Separate Conferences and Seminars on specialist subjects were also attended throughout each year with serious intentions, but occasionally after a hard day's concentration there was a tendency to make it a lively social occasion:

- *A report on the highly educational MRS Winter School, held annually at the Grand Hotel in Eastbourne, described how in one year the 63 delegates and 13 lecturers started with "a formal sherry party of complete strangers" and ended with "a raving disco of permanent friends".*

- *And in the same location, at an MRS Winter School in the 1980s the distinguished Convenor and three colleagues were discovered in the central lobby at about 1.00am engaged in the advanced stages of a game of strip poker. Thankfully the hotel management broke up the party when the Convenor had been reduced to his underpants and about to lose the game entirely.*

International Conferences

Elsewhere, some of the most lively conferences were those convened annually at some European resort by the European professional body, ESOMAR, the first of which was convened in Amsterdam in 1948. Other later locations for this included Paris, Biarritz, Copenhagen, Barcelona, Budapest, Monte Carlo, and in the UK Bristol and Brighton.

In the early days much of the leadership came from Britain, though this too often led to a kind of insensitive arrogance:

- *The report on the Budapest Conference commented: "One cannot defend the number of British speakers who gabble too fast for the interpreters, make no attempt to relate their delivered papers to a wider European audience, and use abbreviations and slang unintelligible beyond Calais" Too often they referred to various UK bodies by their initials only (such as AA, ACORN, AGB, AGM, AIDCOM, AMA, APG, AQRP,SRA, SRG, SSRC, U&A, and VDU), leaving their mainly European listeners very confused.*

- *At the 1972 ESOMAR Congress in Cannes, a 'notorious incident' was heatedly debated at the ESOMAR AGM afterwards. A senior British researcher chairing a particular session had apparently incensed the French by deciding, via a show of hands, that it should be conducted in English. The cry went up: "How dare the French be forced to speak a foreign language in their own country!" But one leading French delegate shrugged and said "What can you do, when the French for 'marketing' is 'le marketing'?"*

Much of the business of the delegates in trading information on recruitment, acquisitions, techniques and suppliers was in fact conducted away from the conference sessions and around the swimming pool. And these conferences also provided an opportunity to sample the restaurants and other delights of the resort's town centre:

- *Passing down the red light district just off the busy 'Ramblas' thoroughfare in Barcelona, one delegate observed the bored-looking ladies of the night and, with his mind full of that day's conference papers on corporate strategy, remarked "In all seriousness, they are doing a very bad job of marketing the meat market".*

- *At the ESOMAR Congress in Rome in 1984, delegates attended a grand Papal Audience lasting three and a half hours, which Pope John Paul II addressed in nine languages. A leading British researcher summed up the occasion by saying: "That was wonderful. But it was rather like a lot of ESOMAR papers – I didn't understand most of it and it went on rather long, but it would have been rude to leave before the end."*

Europe:

It has always been true, especially in the early days of the industry, that the UK was among the most prominent centres for the coordination of multi-country surveys. These would most often be across Europe, where client-organisation and research-supplier colleagues so often seemed to conform to their national stereotypes: the Germans were very formal, never greeting each other with their first names and never flexible enough to take up Plan B when it was obvious to all other countries that Plan A, hatched in New York, was headed for disaster; the French always applied intelligent original thinking, but gummed up the works by saying 'Zis will not work in France'; and as for the British, our European colleagues said we tended to assume that endlessly talking about the issues was in itself an achievement, while not actually executing the job in hand.

And there are always language difficulties to contend with:

> • *At the start of a meeting in Germany of Americans, Brits and Germans to discuss research on a pharmaceutical product, the American boss tried to call the meeting to order. But two Germans continued talking despite a stunned silence among the rest. When they finally stopped, one of them apologised and said he could not stop his more senior colleague. As is common in German grammar, it was a long sentence and he was 'waiting for the verb'.*

> • *In Holland, the simultaneous translation of a focus group discussion met with a problem when the Dutch interpreter refused to translate comments by one participant because "I hate that man. His views are totally right wing. I'm not telling you what he said."*

> • *And in Norway the local interpreter was very laid back and was seen texting on his phone. When accosted, he excused himself by saying "Many Scandinavians talk quite slowly."*

- *At a briefing on research on gemstones, the results were being presented (in French) by an extremely talented and professional French man. The problem was that he was putting his charts up, too high in the projector and on the screen. So a young English executive in the audience asked in her best French "Please could you lower the chart? This was followed by a stony silence, as the presenter dropped his jaw.*

  This silence was broken by a young Canadian lady present: "Did you want him to lower the chart, because you have actually just asked him if he would sleep with you?"

The enhanced role of women in research was at first not easily accepted in some parts of Europe:

- *When four European companies within a group belonging to a British company were asked to accept a reporting line that went straight to the UK headquarters, which was then headed by the formidable Eileen Cole (the first woman to be elected Chair of the MRS), it was not universally welcomed. During the formal round-table meeting in Paris at which she briefed everyone on the new arrangements, the head of the French company was especially put out. But instead of protesting vocally, he simply unravelled his long De Gaulle-like frame, strolled over to the wall and silently executed a perfect handstand. The meeting continued uninterrupted while he remained there for some time, ignored by everyone else. And eventually he unravelled himself from the vertical axis and returned to the table without a word.*

The capacity for international misunderstanding is further illustrated by this famous story:

> • Under pressure from domestic feminist organisations, a Swedish multinational telexed its subsidiaries in other countries: 'Please report number of employees broken down by age and sex'. From a far-flung outpost of the corporate empire came the reply: "The number is zero. Our main problem is alcohol".

And this also illustrates what can happen to the life in research when abroad:

> • In the mid-eighties, most products in Eastern Europe were relatively very cheap, but foreign products such as Johnnie Walker and Chivas Regal whisky were extremely hard to get and very expensive. In Budapest, a Johnnie Walker director researching the markets there decided to visit with colleagues a very select casino bar, expecting cheap prices but armed with a $100 note. Having ordered and received two shots of his own brand of whisky, he put his $100 note in the waitress' tray. To his surprise, she reacted rather grumpily, and colleagues had to explain to him that he had paid just enough for the whiskies _without_ the customarily excessive tip.

> • In the early 1980s, a multinational study for a large computer firm was undertaken, and its initial briefing meeting for everyone involved was convened in Nice by the client. After the meeting, the client invited the entire group to dinner at a seafront restaurant which to everyone's surprise was inhabited by a large number of glamorous women in glitzy ball gowns. It became clear that this was Nice's premier transvestite lounge.
>
> On the way back to the hotel, the client suddenly said he had left his wallet at the restaurant. He turned back, saying he would catch up later and meet everyone in the hotel bar. But he was not seen until the next morning.

Russia

A picture of the hazards of conducting research in Russia in the decade after 'Glasnost' (i.e.1990s) is provided by a leading UK researcher, who was conducting interviews throughout Europe for the 'Eurowinter Project':

- *This was designed to establish how people dealt with cold weather, and its impact on mortality (and incidentally the results from it were very influential, were published in the Lancet and the British Medical Journal, and it is still cited today).*

  He arrived with a colleague in Ekaterinburg in the Urals at midnight, having been warned of the 'criminality situation' in the city and they were directed to a large building surrounded by a security fence, with guards "roaming in the murk of a chemical smog" who had been employed by local residents to protect them and their homes from robbers. Eventually they gained entry and found it had been an eye hospital in an area surrounded by military installations which had suffered contamination from the explosion of an experimental anthrax weapon. This was where they stayed while conducting interviews during the days which followed.

  A year later they were required to confirm their findings by a visit to Yakutsk in Siberia, the world's coldest city with temperatures on their arrival of -35c. A series of bribes were needed to secure permission to continue their work, in a town where most people wore ankle-length coats and fur hats, with a high incidence of frostbite and drunkenness. And they flew home in an ancient-looking Tupolev aircraft which "looked as if it was held together by string."

Earlier, in 1983, the celebrated head of Gallup UK described his recent visit to Russia:

> • *He was surprised to find that the Institute for Sociological*
> *Research, responsible for the majority of the social surveys*
> *in the Soviet Union, conducted 20-25 studies each year.*
> *Topics included attitudes to family life, job satisfaction,*
> *adult literacy, the impact of Soviet media and even political*
> *studies, – though he added that they do not have our*
> *difficulty in forecasting who will win the elections. The*
> *range of his impressive international clientele was*
> *demonstrated to visitors to his London office, where the*
> *walls were decorated with signed photos of Margaret*
> *Thatcher, Ronald Reagan, Pope John Paul II, and Mikhail*
> *Gorbachev.*

In the USA

On the basis of 'Who knows England who only England knows', it is well worth incorporating in a research career a period of working elsewhere. The 'elsewhere' which looms larger than anywhere else is America. But when you get there, you can be confronted by several surprises. If you are offered the flattering title of Vice President by the Chairman of your new company you may imagine that you are thereby number two in his pecking order, but on arrival you may find that the company has six other Vice Presidents, and above them, four Senior Vice Presidents, and two Executive Vice Presidents. (At the Chase Manhattan Bank in the 1970s there were 257 Vice Presidents, and a Managing Director instead of being the Chief Executive of any enterprise, is junior to the most lowly Vice President).

Such transatlantic misunderstandings have to be carefully avoided:

- *When the Chairman of a leading American research company addressed the assembled staff of the British subsidiary he had just acquired, he declared to them how good it was to see them 'on the job', to much muffled mirth. But in New York, when offering to collect a female colleague on the way to a client meeting the next morning it is best not to say "Shall I knock you up in the morning?"*

- *Again, in the early eighties, an American client, inexperienced in international research, commissioned a pan-European study and this was coordinated by the director of a British research company. When he was confronted with 17 different translations of the questionnaire, he was dumbfounded as he had assumed that everyone in Europe spoke English. Once he had been disabused of this, he swung to other end of the spectrum and decided that nobody in Europe spoke English. And so it was that the American client found himself in a conference room in Paris, for a briefing of all the national field managers on the study. "Dick", he roared across the room to the Briton. "France – such a beautiful country, but the people – such assholes!" All around the conference table the murmur arose. "Qu'est-ce que c'est asshole?"*

- *More recently, in the 1990s General Motors were hugely excited about the launch of their new-generation Cadillac, but qualitative research along with 'Car Clinic' test drives found that every respondent thought the visual designs of the new 'Caddy' had a character by-pass and were wholly unappealing. But they were captivated by the array of high-tech innovations in the car, including a satellite-driven communications capability and infra-red night vision.*

  At the research debrief in Detroit, where the results were delivered by an experienced British researcher, the big American chief from Cadillac, still wedded to the visual design, didn't want to hear that being rubbished in favour of the new clever technology. He immediately demanded that the researcher presenting his findings should be silenced and escorted from the building.

  That 'Caddy' was a failure but its technical innovations have been the hugely successful feature of every new Cadillac model since then.

- *An American multinational advertising agency planned a European meeting of the heads of all their European offices. Their pre-determined theme required everyone to wear bright green satin baseball jackets, with baseballs thrown at anyone thought to have made a positive contribution to the meeting. Gathering for the group photo afterwards with everyone feeling uncomfortable in their baseball gear, the head of the French office said: "What will I do with this? – I will <u>never</u> wear it again."*

After getting down to work in the USA, you may quickly learn that although the size of the country and of the projects tended to be much larger, technically the UK is equal to or in advance of US everyday research practice. And (as happened to one British researcher) don't be surprised if, in setting up a group research location in Kansas, you are confronted by a large sign saying 'NO HANDGUNS'.

A US federal employment application form contained the following question:

> • *'Do you favour the overthrow of the government by force, subversion or violence?' One applicant thought it was a multiple-choice question and answered 'Violence'.*

After spending time in New York, you may find it worthwhile to make a move to another part of the great republic, and along with Chicago Illinois, California is in the forefront of the states worth considering. In the 1970s, the world's first research company specialising in survey work for the major film studios was set up in Los Angeles, and within eighteen months it had captured 60% of research commissioned by Universal Studios and 25% of Paramount's.

The idea of accompanying movie-making with the techniques of marketing research was something entirely new for the Hollywood film industry, and it has since grown into a significant business activity. Mostly this was through concept-testing movie ideas, determining their distribution strategies, and testing advertisements for new movies after they had been made, but not released.

The most remarkable early project was for the eccentric cattle baron Jack Wrather, a born-again Christian who had bought all the rights to the 'Lassie' movies:

- He was keen to make a new Lassie movie with an uplifting Christian message and at the same time he wanted it to be a musical and a comedy. To make this hotchpotch a reality he recruited James Stewart (to play Grandad), Mickey Rooney (to provide comedy) and the famous singer Pat Boone's daughter Debbie (who had a rising career as a pop singer).

When they had nearly finished making the movie, the researchers were called in by the Wrather Corporation to help plan its advertising and promotion. What should its title be? Which of its stars had the greatest pulling power? Should it be aimed at kids, their parents or their grandparents? Should it be positioned as a musical, a comedy, a 'message' movie, or an adventure movie?

- *A number of surveys were undertaken, mostly by telephone across the whole USA, and the results indicated that the title, tested against five other possibilities, was to be "The Magic of Lassie," and on the awareness and appeal of each of the stars appearing in it, the answer (as could have been predicted without the research) was that Lassie beat all human rivals: it was a <u>Dog</u> Movie, and an adventure to be aimed at kids.*

  For this piece of insight, the researchers were paid handsomely. And this tended to be true for all similar movie projects: they were mostly produced and directed by young men not yet aged 30, with a budget in excess of $25 million. They hardly cared whether they were charged $50,000 or $500,000 for the research – it was small change to them.

The confident assertiveness of some American clients is illustrated by this story:

- *In 1982, a British research company was contacted by a US contact lens maker who wanted to study the Japanese market. Their representative was a marketer who had never conducted research outside America. He wanted an omnibus survey done but didn't want any analysis or a report – just the data. He received the results in a report with a nice binder, but a few days later, he made a phone call to the leading executive in the British company. "Great work!" he bellowed "Just one question: what does DK/CR mean? It's on every damn table!" "Don't know/Can't remember", the Briton replied. To which the American's response was "Well, if you don't know, who the hell does?"*

Elsewhere

Further afield, a research career can offer many opportunities to travel and learn about other countries.

Iran

In some parts of the world the life expectancy of British research companies setting up there can be short. For instance, in Iran the downfall of the Shah in 1979 meant that one new UK company there had to shut up shop rather quickly:

- *Before that, on arrival for a first visit to Iran, the UK-based Director in charge was diverted at Passport Control to a cramped windowless cell for an interrogation by the Shah's Savak secret police. Eventually he was released, helped by the intervention of his local colleagues.*

  Then, when setting up a joint national study for the BBC, he was stopped from doing that after being told the BBC had 'insulted' the Shah.

  Much later, when the Shah had been deposed, it became clear the UK company's Iranian venture would have to be closed. This became most evident when their branch of the Irano-British bank was burned down.

Latin America:

At an AMA/MRS (Anglo-American) seminar a well-informed speech was delivered on the subject of market research in Latin America:

> • *"Revolutions are not really a problem. You stay indoors for a day or two and then it is back to normal." He also warned that one should not use the normal buying scale question among Latinos. "The lowest point on the scale must be 'I will buy it' with the top point being 'I certainly will buy and pay for it'. Apart from that, he reckoned Latinos were just the same as everyone else, except that income information is totally, but totally, unreliable."*

Saudi Arabia:

The necessity to acknowledge local conditions arose when a British research company was asked to organise in Saudi Arabia a product test on a brand of ice cream:

> • *Large quantities of the product were air-lifted from the UK but, having been unloaded on arrival it was left in its container on the runway in searing heat for two days. Of course, when opened the ice cream had irretrievably melted. So they had to order a replacement, and this time it was deeply packaged within a thick layer of ice around the ice cream, which solved the problem.*

China:

In 1987, one of our leading qualitative researchers gave her impressions of the third World Advertising Congress in Beijing, with sentiments which could largely hold true today:

> • *"Everything was on a mammoth scale, from the auditorium seating 1,500 to the banquet in a room resembling a football pitch ... One dish consisted of jellyfish and sea cucumber (not a vegetable but a very large marine slug).*
>
> *Sea slugs aside, there were lots of good moments in the five-day conference, for example rent-a-delegate locals were apparently brought in off the street at the last moment to compensate for a shortfall in numbers, and a little group of Chinese laughed their way through endless re-runs of the Benny Hill Show in preference to other programmes on offer at the Thames Television stall.*
>
> *Most of the papers seemed to have a disregard for intellectual content, and the potential wall-to-wall flow of 'creative excellence from around the world' (ie commercials) was only impeded by the need to have very long, slow, official speeches from Chinese officials. Now I know why their culture is 4,000 years old."*

Another lesson was learned in China when focus group participants were asked to switch off their phones, and they all did so:

> • *The reason for this request was partly that the purpose of the research was to test reactions to the client's highly confidential new drink, of which a bottle was visible to all on the table. Later, when the moderator briefly left the room, the participants quickly photographed it with their <u>other</u> phones, and posted it on social media. She had not realised that it was common for young people in China to own two or three phones.*

Japan:

In a report on the Japan Marketing Association Conference, one British delegate wrote:

- *"The lack of questions from the floor is not unusual in Japanese meetings, since matters of substance have been worked out privately prior to the meeting. Thus the person who asks questions at a meeting is either a troublemaker or a person not important enough to be consulted in advance."*

A UK research company conducting a multi-country survey for a leading international accountancy firm asked a local Japanese research company to undertake the Japanese interviewing:

- *One of its British executives was sent there to make the arrangements, and after a day of discussion in Tokyo he was taken out to dinner by the head of the Japanese research company.*

  Halfway through the meal the Japanese CEO stiffened, drew himself upright and apologetically stated:

  "There is something I must tell you. I am not Japanese."
  "Oh, that's no problem.
  "So where are you from?"
  "My family are from China".
  "That's fine. And when did they come over from China?"
  "It was four hundred years ago."

  Which tells us a lot about the closed culture of Japan: after 400 years, he was still 'not Japanese.'

Nevertheless Japan sometimes provided opportunities for unbridled mischief:

> • *A British research executive on a similar visit to the country felt unable to reject an invitation to visit a businessman's lap dancing bar, where his local manager enticed him into special engagement with the performers.*
>
> *Guilt ridden on the following day, he elicited promises from his colleagues that nothing would get back to his HQ in the UK. Unfortunately on his return home he found in his office a blow-up doll sitting in his chair.*

India:

One of the many benefits of a career involving international research is the opportunity to learn and sympathise more fully with different ways of looking on life and its problems. In India, expectations that survey research could be conducted straightforwardly have to be abandoned when it is realised that most nationwide survey questionnaires have to be translated into at least seventeen major languages, and a proportion of respondents do not have the literacy skills to consider a card showing a written choice of answers.

The unfamiliarity of some American clients with life outside their own country seemed apparent in too many projects in the past, if not now:

> • *One such client refused to leave his hotel room in Calcutta because there were children begging at his window, and he would only eat at McDonald's, even though it was one hour's journey time across town.*

But a different kind of unfamiliarity might sometimes be said of the British:

> • *When a British researcher was asked to set up a series of*
> *teach-in sessions for Indian research executives in*
> *Hyderabad, a state in central India with a Muslim group*
> *ruling a mainly Hindu population, he was warned on the*
> *phone by his intended host before departing that one*
> *could not buy alcoholic drinks in that state. "Not a*
> *problem", he said, "I can do without alcohol for a week".*
> *At which point his more perceptive wife kicked him under*
> *the table and whispered "No – what he means is, for*
> *heaven's sake bring some in". Which he did, and enjoyed*
> *a welcome party arranged for him, with the local police*
> *cruising by, until paid off with a necessary bribe.*

Perhaps to illustrate the commitment of India to a market-based and customer-oriented outlook, in 1981 an article by a director of Research International in India ended with the words that Mahatma Gandhi (no less) had apparently used to describe the importance of the Indian, or any other, customer: "He is not dependent on us, we are dependent on him; he is not an interruption in our work, he is the purpose of it; he is not an outsider in our business, he is part of it."

Africa:

Much earlier, in 1971 a British polling company was asked by Independent Television News to set up a survey of African opinion in Rhodesia (now Zimbabwe) during the time of the white-supremacist Smith regime:

- *On arrival, the British pollster (despite being constantly followed by secret policemen) found there was a competent local field force affiliated to the leading British research organisation, Research International. They had been used to conducting surveys on subjects such as soap powders and foodstuffs, but they bravely took up this highly political project. All went well, using teams of African interviewers who drove off into the distant bush in Land Rovers, needing to secure permission from each village headman. In each village they offered him a cheap BIC biro as an incentive, which was gratefully received. In one very remote village he then removed the long polished stick he kept inserted through his nostrils, and proudly paraded up and down the main street with the BIC biro inserted in its place, for all of his villagers to see and admire.*

  Forty years after independence, such a scene would now be unlikely.

Culture clash in northern Ouagadougou:

- *The researcher was conducting (in French) a test of food products with a group of soft-spoken and charming men, when all of a sudden they got up and left the room. She was left wondering what she had done wrong. But ten minutes later they wandered back into the room, one of them explaining "Sorry lady, we had to go and pray." Lesson learned: choose your time of day carefully.*

Local realities were also apparent to a British interviewer doing research on a well-known beer brand in the remote 'outback' of Tanzania:

> *When her car broke down, she managed to hitch a lift in a truck, and she found herself squeezed between an Irish nun and a Tanzanian priest, with a chicken sitting on her lap. For three hours they rattled down the road singing hymns, while she wondered if the nun, who did the driving, had actually passed a driving test.*

In the business district of Lagos, Nigeria, a very different reality was encountered:

> *Out in the street, a British researcher decided to take a photo of an advertising billboard, not noticing that a group of what turned out to be plain clothes policemen were standing in front of it. They demanded that she should hand over her camera and when she refused, took her to the local police station where they said she must pay a fine. Since she didn't have any money with her there was a long stand-off, resolved eventually when her local minder and research recruiter turned up, and spoke to a man behind the counter. Money was exchanged and he called a taxi which took her away to safety.*

And the gulf between ill-informed western expectations and African realities was further demonstrated by a creative development research project conducted in Burkino Faso for an American cigarette manufacturer:

- *This landlocked country is a thousand miles from the sea, very poor and remote. As required in the research, a group was convened of eight eager and engaging young men aged 20-34 who were all heavy smokers. They were shown a series of billboards depicting an aspirational, western, glamorous lifestyle with pictures of a glorious ocean, very fancy yacht, fabulous beach and sleek (white) men, with the punch line "Everything you wished for."*

Their reactions were not as expected by the client: "He's been on a long journey. Must be very tired." "He has been travelling to the big water – it's a long way, takes maybe a month, costs a lot of money and a lot of shoes. Not safe too."

Another said "He is so brave, hanging out over the boat and fishing. I wouldn't want to do that, I can't swim, this white person is nuts, he will die."

So the moderator asked "So what is this advertising telling you?"

The response: "You are nuts and you are going to die. You will have no fish for your family; your family will be sad and you will be poor."

5.   A MATURING INDUSTRY

Technical Changes

In recent years the characteristics of an industry entering the mature phase of the product lifecycle have begun to appear.

There is less emphasis on invention, and more on maintenance and tracking procedures, all aided by the cheap facilities of massive databases, in which technical fastidiousness is less assured and low sampling response rates are readily accepted. In 1973, one leading fieldwork company could claim that in a survey involving 10,000 voters selected from the electoral registers, a response rate of 85% had been achieved. Nowadays, very few surveys achieve more than a 50% response, and among internet-based surveys it is usually less than 10%.

However the industry is now engaged in a broader range of activities than was previously the case. From a survey of the industry by MrWeb in 2017 we learn that the most important trends are thought to be the integration of MR with other data (54%), story-telling in research presentations (43%) and dealing with the government's GDPR regulations. In the previous 12 months, 88% had used on-line surveys, 60% had used focus groups, 55% telephone interviews, and 55% in-depth face-to face interviews (so clearly qualitative research is not in decline). But only 23% had used face-to-face quantitative surveys, which in previous decades had been the mainstay of the industry.

© D.Fletcher for CloudTweaks.com

The first warning signs from the integration of market research into the broader information industry were given as long ago as 1985 with one leading researcher writing that "this will bring a number of problems, especially in relation to data quality whose minimum standards have so far been safeguarded by the Market Research Society Code of Conduct. Market research data will sit alongside other data on linked electronic databases where there is no independent guarantee of quality". Another senior researcher commented "In a world where data are plentiful and their collection is automated, it will become increasingly difficult to ensure standards are maintained".

Nonetheless the advantages of speed and low cost cannot be denied: it is clear that technology in the form of digital advancements in data collection, analysis and distribution is the key driver determining how research will contribute to decision making in the future.

> • *An illustration of the change taking place in the research industry was provided by a 1982 visit to the husband-and-wife founders of the well-established Infratest Institute in Germany, the two Drs Ernst. Seeing themselves as social scientists, they greeted the UK researchers wearing white coats as though they were scientific laboratory technicians. More recently, with the growth of big data and continuous monitoring studies it seems more appropriate that some industry leaders should instead wear the <u>brown</u> coats of factory managers.*

Career Fulfilment

A piece of advice can be provided here for those who are intending to enter the research business, and those already in it: as part of their preparation for a role in general management, a leading multinational company sent a group of promising employees to a series of lectures at INSEAD, the European Business School. The most memorable talk during their three weeks there was by John Evans of the HR faculty, who explained that to be happy in your work you need to be ...

- **Good at** what you do, otherwise you are a *competence* misfit,
- **Enjoy** what it involves, otherwise you are an *enjoyment* misfit,
- **Believe** in what you are doing, otherwise you are a *moral* misfit.

This struck home: within six months, several of those attending that lecture had left the company they worked for. But they quickly found many other avenues in both research and marketing for their talents to develop happily.

It has long been suggested that although researchers may be technically proficient, they are mostly not so good at holding their own among top decision makers in major corporate boardrooms:

> • *In 1973, one leading client from an advertising agency asserted "I want researchers who are significant in the sense that people pay attention to them in a crunchy meeting."*

Some researchers progress happily in their careers by demonstrating excellence in executing research, but to reach the top one must move on from project management and learn how to manage people and organisations. And in the long run, if one has set up or managed a business successfully, there comes a time when one must consider one's exit route by organising succession management and handing over to the next generation, or by selling the business to a willing buyer. Not everyone achieves these outcomes and some retire to live on little more than their pensions.

A distinguished President of the Society could say in 1966 with some truth that "Market research has been a tremendous growth industry, but it is a pity that, like so many other growth industries, there is no real money to be made out of it." Increasingly in the years since then, this has become untrue: many research companies have grown and been sold, merged or handed on to the next generation with the original owners pocketing large sums and enjoying an easy retirement.

> • *But not everyone wants to take that high-powered route: as one chief of a smaller company said: "When our accountant asked what our objectives were, we simply said "To be happy." And when he asked "But don't you want to grow?" we said again "No, we don't want to be corporate managers, just to be happy."*

"They come and go. I've outlasted five of them."

For several superannuated researchers, a career in the industry is not the end of the road. Looking back from 2003, creating a new life after (or even before) retiring were:

2 Expert Witnesses in Legal Cases
2 Masters of the Worshipful Company of Marketors
3 Lecturers on Cruise Ships
5 Who gained further qualifications and distinctions in Academia.

Others said they worked for Charities, took up Painting, became Expert in Crossword Compiling, did lectures for the U3A, went into Pig Farming, and 3 said they simply had lunch and laughter with friends.

And in 2009 some of the Postgraduate Degrees reported to have been obtained by recently retired researchers were:

MA in Arts Market Appraisal from Kingston University.

MA in English Literature (with Distinction) from the Open University.

MA in Anthropology (with Distinction) from the School of Oriental and African Studies (SOAS).

Advanced Certificate with the Wine and Spirits Educational Trust.

"Oh, come dear. You had a good run. You've stayed overrated for far longer than I thought you would."

Consultancy:

But ahead of that, the increasing focus of one's later career can be on providing consultancy advice. Too often researchers charge too little for that, especially compared with other professionals such as lawyers and management consultants:

> • *As an example of that from 20 years ago, when completing*
> *a worldwide project for the leading accountancy firm*
> *Price Waterhouse, the coordinating researcher was asked*
> *to stay on as a consultant. He then suggested that he*
> *might want to charge £1,000 a day for his time. But this*
> *prompted the following response from the firm's research*
> *manager: "For heaven's sake double it, otherwise my*
> *colleagues (regularly charging their accountancy clients*
> *£2,000+) will think you're no good". So he did, hoping to*
> *foster a belief that advice from researchers is as valuable*
> *as it is from other types of consultant.*

And if you are categorised by your client as a consultant, you can capture the attention of their management team much more forcefully than if you are an employee. One such consultant working for a leading bank found himself at a meeting, chatting in an easy manner with a senior director he did not know and listened to attentively, – which would never happened if he had been one of the bank's employees, constrained by hierarchical conventions.

Links to Academia:

Throughout these years it has been true that, unlike the situation in the USA where the universities are at the forefront of the intellectual development of survey research, in the UK contacts with academia have been rare and new thinking has mostly been driven by the research suppliers. At a meeting in 1973 the Managing Director of Gallup UK expressed a concern that relations between the market research industry and the academic world were not at the right status level. He felt the Market Research Society was working well with polytechnics but there was far too little liaison with universities, where market research was largely ignored both as an industry and as a useful tool for furthering knowledge in a number of faculties.

The AMSR:

Happily, this problem is not so severe, helped at least in part, by the launch in 2016 of the Archive of Market and Social Research (www amsr.org.uk). While the research companies seem preoccupied with their current and future problems, the universities and their students are showing great interest in using this new Archive to reinforce their understanding of social and commercial trends, and the research industry and its history.

This is being done with the blessing of the Market Research Society which, throughout one's career should be your central reference point for matters to do with technical expertise and professional standards. You may change your job several times, being a supplier, a buyer or an independent consultant at differing times, but the Society will always be there for you. Whatever challenges it may face in future, its central role in guiding individual researchers and the industry as a whole should remain undiminished.